FITNESS ESTIMATION USING ARTIFICIAL INTELLIGENCE

PRANALI DHAWAS

BHARGAVI KAKIRWAR, TANMAY HANDE, AADITYA GUPTA

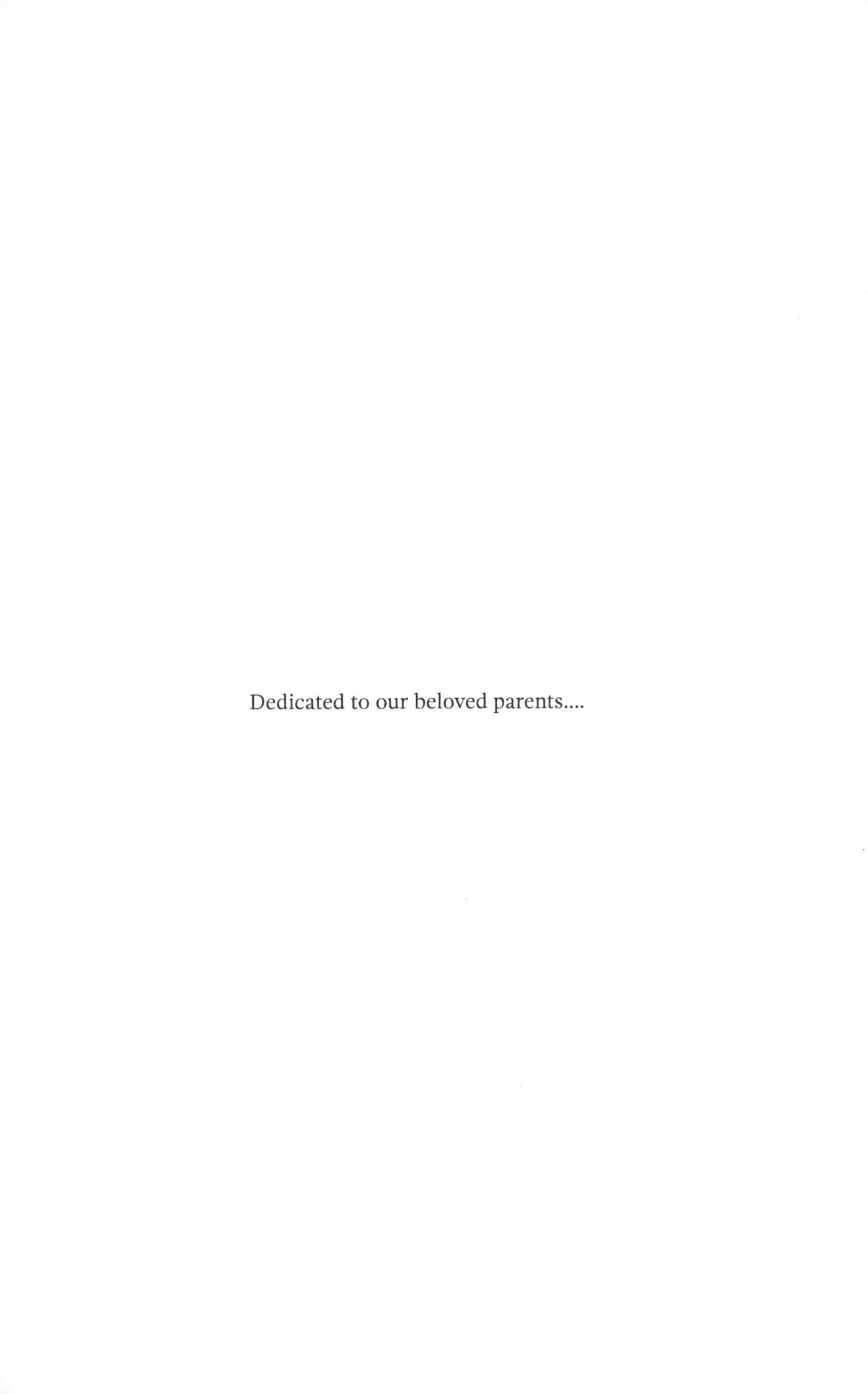

Dedicated to our beloved parents....

Contents

Content

Foreword

In an era where technology is rapidly advancing, the fusion of artificial intelligence and fitness has become a promising frontier. "Fitness Estimation Using Artificial Intelligence" ventures into this exciting domain, offering insights into how cutting-edge techniques can revolutionize the way we approach workout routines and injury prevention.

Strength training, undoubtedly effective for physical development, often poses challenges, particularly for newcomers who face the risk of injuries due to improper form. Addressing this concern, this book delves into the realm of artificial intelligence, harnessing its power to provide real-time feedback on workout techniques. By leveraging the advancements in deep learning and human pose estimation, the authors propose a groundbreaking approach to analyze and enhance exercise performance.

The journey outlined in these pages unfolds with meticulous attention to detail, presenting a comprehensive exploration of the intersection between fitness and technology. Through rigorous research and experimentation, the authors unveil a feedback system capable of detecting technique-related issues with remarkable precision. Their findings not only showcase the potential of artificial intelligence in improving workout efficacy but also underscore the importance of tailored feedback in injury prevention and performance optimization.

Central to this discourse is the comparative analysis of deep learning models, offering invaluable insights into their efficacy in recognizing and classifying various workout routines. With an impressive accuracy score of 97.25 percent achieved in validation, the authors demonstrate the robustness of their approach, laying a solid foundation for future advancements in the field.

Moreover, the book offers a critical evaluation of existing human pose estimation systems, shedding light on their effectiveness in detecting technique-related issues across diverse exercises and user profiles. While acknowledging the challenges posed by certain filming perspectives, the authors highlight the promising strides made in this domain, emphasizing the need for further exploration and refinement.

As readers embark on this enlightening journey, they are invited to witness the convergence of fitness and artificial intelligence, poised to reshape the landscape of exercise science. "Fitness Estimation Using

Artificial Intelligence" serves as a beacon of innovation, inspiring researchers, practitioners, and enthusiasts alike to embrace the transformative potential of technology in pursuit of optimal health and performance.

Preface

In the realm of fitness and exercise, the quest for improvement is often met with challenges, particularly for newcomers navigating the complexities of technique and form. The journey towards mastering strength training or yoga, while undeniably rewarding, can also be fraught with the risk of injury. As every individual embarks on this path, they encounter their own set of hurdles and obstacles, necessitating personalized feedback tailored to their unique needs.

Against this backdrop, recent advancements in deep learning and the availability of vast datasets have paved the way for groundbreaking applications across diverse industries, from automotive to healthcare. However, the integration of deep learning technologies into the realm of sports, fitness, and injury rehabilitation has remained relatively uncharted territory, presenting a ripe opportunity for innovation.

This book chronicles a pioneering exploration into the fusion of human pose estimation technology with fitness training—a marriage of cutting-edge artificial intelligence with the timeless pursuit of physical excellence. Grounded in a foundation of meticulous research and driven by a relentless commitment to progress, this endeavor seeks to revolutionize the way we approach workout feedback.

The journey begins where the seeds of innovation were sown. Through a meticulous examination of deep learning models and the harnessing of extensive datasets, the groundwork was laid for the development of a feedback system poised to revolutionize the fitness landscape. Phase 1 laid the groundwork for what was to come, establishing the framework upon which future progress would be built.

As you delve into the pages that follow, prepare to embark on a journey of discovery and innovation. From the intricacies of deep learning algorithms to the practical applications of human pose estimation technology, each chapter offers new insights and revelations. Together, let us venture into uncharted territory, where the boundaries of possibility are limited only by the scope of our imagination.

Welcome to the future of fitness. Welcome to a world where technology and tradition converge to unlock the full potential of the human body. Welcome to a revolution in workout feedback.

Acknowledgements

This book on "Fitness Estimation using Artificial Intelligence" would not have been possible without the contributions and support of numerous individuals and organizations, to whom I extend my heartfelt gratitude.

I would also like to express my appreciation to the Department of Artificial Intelligence, G H Raisoni College of Engineering, Nagpur for providing the necessary resources and facilities that facilitated our research efforts. Your support has been indispensable in bringing this project to fruition.

Last but not least, I am grateful to my family and friends for their unwavering encouragement, understanding, and patience throughout this journey. Your love and support have been my source of strength and motivation.

Together, we have embarked on a remarkable journey to explore the intersection of fitness and artificial intelligence, and I am deeply grateful to each one of you for being part of this endeavor

Prologue

In the realm where technology intersects with the pursuit of physical excellence, a revolution is underway-a revolution born from the marriage of deep learning algorithms and human pose estimation technology. It is a revolution that holds the promise of transforming the way we approach fitness, offering a beacon of hope to newcomers and seasoned athletes alike.

At its core lies a simple truth: while strength training and yoga offer myriad benefits, they also present a significant risk of injury, particularly for those just beginning their fitness journey. Yet, amidst this challenge lies an opportunity to leverage the power of artificial intelligence to provide real-time, personalized feedback, guiding individuals toward safer and more effective workouts.

This book chronicles the culmination of years of research, innovation, and collaboration-a journey that began with a simple question: could technology be harnessed to enhance the way we approach fitness? Phase 1 of this project laid the groundwork, exploring the potential of deep learning models and large datasets to revolutionize workout feedback. It was a time of discovery, as the team unearthed the untapped potential of human pose estimation technology in the realm of fitness.

Phase 2 represents the next chapter in this journey book characterized by refinement and innovation. Building upon the foundation laid in Phase 1, the team delved deeper into the intricacies of human pose estimation, developing a feedback system capable of providing actionable insights into workout techniques. Through rigorous testing and analysis, they sought to validate the efficacy of this approach, paving the way for a new era in fitness technology.

As you embark on this journey through the pages that follow, prepare to be inspired. From the intricacies of algorithmic design to the practical applications of human pose estimation technology, each chapter offers new insights and revelations. Yet, beyond the technical details lies a deeper story—a story of innovation, of collaboration, and the profound impact that technology can have on our lives.

This is more than just a book it is a testament to the power of human ingenuity and the endless possibilities that lie at the intersection of fitness and technology. It is a call to action—a call to harness the power of innovation to build a brighter, safer, and more inclusive future for fitness enthusiasts around the globe.

Welcome to the future of fitness. Welcome to a world where technology and tradition converge to unlock the full potential of the human body. Welcome to a revolution in workout feedback.

CHAPTER ONE

INTRODUCTION

1.1 PROJECT BACKGROUND

In today's society, the times are constantly developing, and people's requirements for material life will gradually improve. At the same time, people began to pursue a healthy lifestyle, which basically involves physical exercise. Various exercises such as deadlifts, squats, and shoulder presses are favorable to human body fitness, but they can also be very harmful if the exercises are performed improperly. Injuries to the muscles or ligaments can be caused by the heavy weights involved in these exercises. Due to a lack of training or knowledge, many people do not follow the correct posture to be maintained while performing these exercises regularly.

This may lead to muscle fatigue and muscle strain. In this course project, using the latest techniques in pose estimation, we help people perform exercises with correct posture by developing a project that detects the user's pose while exercising, provides feedback, and suggests improvements if necessary. Most weightlifting injuries occur as a result of using incorrect form while performing individual exercises. The most popular of these among strength enthusiasts are the barbell bench press, squat, and deadlift. It just so happens that these exercises in particular are some of the easiest to perform improperly, and as a result, they can be quite dangerous.

The study of human body movement, has played a major role in human lifestyles. Ranging from simply preventing and rehabilitating injured body parts to improving athletic performance by following rigorous training routines. Initially, these tasks were overseen by a coach or a physical therapist. However, improvements in technology have allowed individuals to track their own improvement by using sensory devices that provide feedback data. For example, the Apple Watch initially uses an accelerometer to track step count and calculate how many calories an individual burns.

Beast is another product that also tracks exercises using accelerometers, gyroscopes, and compasses. The field of computer vision has had many breakthroughs in real-world applications.

By incorporating machine learning techniques, many have begun applying the image recognition approaches for pose estimation or action recognition in videos. Pose estimation is used to identify humans in videos, and by taking it one step further, they map out joints from the body and are able to connect the joints to form a skeletal representation. There is an iOS app known as Kaia Squat Challenge, which uses the phone's camera to track 16 points on the body and calculate angles using the relative positions of the limbs. There was also a separate study on action recognition in hockey. In this, they classified four different poses that were identified in a video recording of a hockey game. Although these techniques are fairly new, they have attracted a lot of attention and interest, with much development already in progress.

The ImageNet dataset was an important cornerstone in building image classification models. With over 14 million images and 20,000 labels, it is used for the ImageNet Large Scale Visual Recognition Competition (ILSVRC). The AlexNet model had achieved an error rate below 20%, while others were stuck between 20 and 30. The reason why AlexNet was so successful was that it used a deeper model than those used previously. These results in machine learning, along with the massive amounts of data, sparked interest in many companies, leading to tremendous amounts of investment in research and development in computer vision. Facebook has had major breakthroughs in identifying individuals in group pictures, and Tesla has been constantly improving its self-driving car using image recognition and collecting data through LIDAR sensors.

Our goal with this project is to build a solution that can help users fix their own form and learn to perform these lifts correctly. Incorrect forms have become an increasingly problematic issue in the wake of COVID. Gyms are hotspots for viral transmission, and many beginners are electing to start their fitness journeys at home. However, without feedback from a personal trainer and minimal prior experience, it can be quite a difficult task to learn how to lift weights properly.

1.2 PROBLEM STATEMENT

The goal of the thesis is to build a multitask system including 2D human pose estimation, 2D exercise recognition and counting for exercises based on videos. Detectio n-based 2D pose estimation methods normally get better estimation accuracy, and the byproduct heatmaps contain rich pose location and body shape information. However, a single heat map is meaningless as it only represents one joint's location in a particular frame. Simply tiling all the heatmaps in one video would result in a huge input feature map which requires a complicated model. Therefore, how to process the heatmaps to a small-scale feature map that contains enough joint motion information is a challenging task.

Most off-the-shelf datasets don't support human exercise recognition and repetitive counting multitask. Action recognition dataset like UCF-101 and Penn Action include exercises, but there are no counting labels available. Datasets tailed to repetitive counting like QUVA are short of data regarding exercises. In this case, generating a dataset that includes a variety of repetitive exercises with both action type and counting labels is a big challenge for us. The dataset should also take factors like body moving speeds, different cycles and action continuity into consideration.

Another challenge is the multitask model network. Exercise recognition and counting networks can not be placed in series because neither task leverages the output of the other one. Meanwhile, both tasks can learn from body joint movement information. Therefore, we can build a multitask model by applying a parallel architecture. Global features can be shared between these two networks. In addition, Exercise recognition is considered as a classification problem while counting is regarded as a regression problem. Both tasks are complicated, and strong feature extraction networks should be applied. In summary, the challenges of this thesis are concluded as follows:

The detection-based pose estimation methods generate heatmaps which include numerous motion information. It's necessary to keep the joint motion information while processing the heatmaps into small feature maps.

The available datasets for action recognition or repetitive counting are not suitable for 2D exercise recognition and counting multitask. A new dataset should be created to contain continuous daily exercises. Various action speeds and periods should be taken into account.

A parallel multitask model should be designed for 2D exercise recognition and repetition counting. Powerful feature extraction backbones should be selected for both tasks.

1.3 PURPOSE OF STUDY
OBJECTIVES:

Gain insight in different state-of-the-art approaches for human pose estimation and pick several candidates to evaluate on.

Explore aspects of technique in weightlifting considered to have a high risk of injury and pick the best features with respect to technique variations and body composition to evaluate on.

Produce exercise videos where the chosen technique aspects are present as well as videos where none technique aspects are present. Then generate datasets to be used for testing and evaluation by running the videos on the human pose estimation systems.

Develop a system to detect which exercise is being performed by the subject and from which angle the video is filmed, so that technique aspects from that particular exercise and view can be automatically tested for.

Develop universal formulas with a high likelihood of detecting technique aspects associated with risk for the common user.

Analyze the findings and compare the different pose estimators against each other. Evaluate the system's ability to recognize filming angle and exercise, as well as its ability to detect individual technique errors.

1.4 TECHNOLOGICAL BASE

This project can be implemented by using various technologies like:

OpenCV:

OpenCV is an open-source Python library, which is used to understand the content of the digital image. The CV is the abbreviation form of computer vision. It extracts the description from the real-time image or digital image and performs many tasks such as face detection, face recognition, blob detection, edge-detection, image filter, template matching, and etc.

NumPy:

NumPy is a library for the Python programming language, adding support for large, multi dimensional arrays and matrices, along with a large collection of high-level mathematical functions to operate on these arrays.

Pandas:

Pandas is a software library written for the Python programming language for data manipulation and analysis. In particular, it offers data structures and operations for manipulating numerical tables and time series.

Matplotlib:

Matplotlib is a plotting library for the Python programming language and its numerical mathematics extension NumPy. It provides an object-oriented API for embedding plots into applications using general-purpose

GUI toolkits.

SciKit-Learn:

Scikit-learn is a free software machine learning library for the Python programming language. It features various classification, regression and clustering algorithms.

TensorFlow:

TensorFlow is a free and open-source software library for machine learning and artificial intelligence. It can be used across a range of tasks but has a particular focus on training and inference of deep neural networks.

Keras:

Keras is an open-source software library that provides a Python interface for artificial neural networks. Keras acts as an interface for the TensorFlow library.

OpenPose API:

OpenPose has represented the first real-time multi-person system to jointly detect human body, hand, facial, and foot key points (in total 135 key points) on single images.

MediaPipe:

MediaPipe offers cross-platform, customizable ML solutions for live and streaming media.

PIL:

PIL is the Python Imaging Library which provides the python interpreter with image editing capabilities. PIL.Image.new () method creates a new image with the given mode and size. Size is given as a (width, height)-tuple, in pixels.

Random:

The random module is another library of functions that can extend the basic features of python. Other modules we have seen so far are string, math, time and graphics. With the exception of the graphics module, all of these modules are built into python.

JSON:

JSON is a syntax for storing and exchanging data. JSON is text, written with JavaScript object notation. Python has a built-in package called JSON, which can be used to work with JSON data.

IO:

The IO module provides Python's main facilities for dealing with various types of I/O. There are three main types of I/O: text I/O, binary I/O and raw I/O. These are generic categories, and various backing stores can be used for each of them. A Concrete object belonging to any of these categories is called a file object.

CHAPTER TWO

LITERATURE SURVEY

2.1 RELATED WORK

The motivation for this project comes from the large successs achieved by multiple computer vision and machine learning models. In particular, pose estimation has provided a variety of options with its key-point challenge results. We train models for pose estimation in our project and use the key points provided to analyze the pose of the individual performing the workout and provide simple feedback, such as how many repetitions the individual has completed. We have implemented an alternative approach to provide similar feedback. We train multiple models on individuals performing a given workout rather than analyzing the workout with key points and angles. Then we apply those models to either real-time or pre-recorded videos and give rep counts back to the user.

This chapter outlines some of the models which motivated our work, along with tools which would help us achieve faster results. Our goal is to be able to cover the following steps end to end:

- Dataset Gathering and Data Labeling
- Dataset Pre-Processing
- Model Selection and Building
- Model Training and Validation
- Model Testing
- Model Deployment

2.1.1 2D HUMAN POSE ESTIMATION

The motivation for this project comes from the large successes achieved by multiple computer vision and machine learning models. In particular, pose estimation has provided a variety of options with its key-point challenge results. Xiong et al. [1] in 2020 worked on robust vision-based workout analysis. Test results show the prevalence of their proposed 3D posture assessment over the past ones. It identifies incorrect motions but not the timing of these motions, and hence does not provide timely feedback to users. They could not integrate their model with video tutorials. Yadav et al. [2] in 2019 approached the problem of accurately recognizing various yoga poses using deep learning algorithms. A dataset of six yoga asanas had been created using 15 individuals. A hybrid deep learning model was proposed using CNN and LSTM for yoga recognition on real-time videos; the system can be implemented on a portable device for real-time predictions and self-training.

Yiwen Gu et al. [3] adopted deep learning models for human pose estimation and worked on home-based physical therapy with an interactive computer vision system in 2019. They could not provide users with a side-view option and could not develop an algorithm that gives more detailed feedback on how the patient is doing, instead of giving feedback based on the overall performance. Chen et al. [4] in 2018 incorporated computer vision strategies and proposed a system that examines the practitioner's stance from both front and side perspectives by separating the body shape, skeleton, dominant axes, and points. Improving or even redesigning the methods of feature point detection and assistant axis generation for some poses can make the system more solid.

Chen and Yang [5] created this application to correct users' poses by generating ideal exercise movements. Deep neural networks and OpenPose were used for pose estimation, and machine learning and heuristic-based models were used to calculate performance by comparison. The developed application is only available on the web and runs on GPU powered Windows and Linux computers. Keshari [6] has used OpenCV for image processing and SVM and RCNN for detecting errors. They have created their own dataset for detecting errors, distributed the dataset to understand proper posture, and used SVM and RCNN to detect incorrect posture.

Nagarkoti et al. [7] use a pre-recorded trainer's video using deep learning and OpenCV. For tracking users' body movements, optical flow tracking is used, and dynamic time warping is used to sync trainers and users' body movements. It only corrects user posture; a proper AI assistant for the user should include tracking exercise repetitions, errors, and creating reports. Agrawal et al. [8] used various classification techniques to detect yoga poses, out of which random forest classifiers gave the best results. It detects and identifies various yoga poses using this application; if the accuracy is calculated, the user will be able to track and improve performance.

Pose estimation for single-person and multi-person was performed by Z. Cao [9]. In single person, they perform inference over a combination of local observations on body parts and the spatial dependencies between them. For multi-person scenes, they have used a top down strategy to first detect people and then estimate the pose of each person independently. It works only on images and cannot be used on videos. Kumar et al. [10] proposed to use OpenPose on the client's ongoing and recorded sessions to distinguish the joint areas by utilizing Part Confidence Maps and Part Affinity Fields. Then, based on the difference in angles, feedback is provided to the user. This works only when images are provided by the user; it does not work in real-time.

Chiddarwar et al. [11] collect a single ideal image for obtaining the key points and store it locally in their machine. Then OpenCV is used to predict the 17 essential key points using a pre-trained model, and the distance between each body part is calculated using Euclidean distance. The system only detects the yoga pose and indicates its correctness. Q. Dang et al. conducted a survey on human pose estimation methods in [12]. The single-person estimation is classified into two types: the regression-based approach and the heat map based approach. Multi-person estimation is classified into two categories: top-down approaches and bottom-up approaches. Human pose estimation methods have significantly improved in recent years and can still be improved for use in real-world applications. The speed of algorithms is still too slow for real-time prediction.

In [13], Sajjad et al compared different techniques for human pose recognition to identify which was better by calculating accuracy for each and getting better results so that the implementation of human pose recognition would be correct. Human action recognition is a domain with great potential. The ability to detect and understand the motion of the body has many benefits in sports and exercise [10]. Several years of research in this domain have identified numerous challenges [11]. The main hurdle in action recognition is identifying the posture of the individual within a stipulated time frame. Numerous works of literature propose systems to analyze athletes to improve upon their game, such as in tennis [12], swimming [13], basketball [14, 15], badminton [16], and rugby [17]. Kelly et al. [18] present an analysis tool to identify and rectify the motion of a golf swing. The swing is compared to expert swings to provide lessons on how the swing mechanics need to be adjusted. Yoga pose recognition has recently been started, and research is going on to apply the benefits of pose estimation to asanas. Several of the previous works on pose estimation [19, 20] utilize stick figure models in place of the human body, with assumptions such as the head necessarily lying above the torso and the shoulder joints being higher than the hip joints. Our poses clearly show such assumptions do not always hold.

Patil et al. [21] introduce a SURF (speeded-up robust features) algorithm to detect the yoga pose performed by comparing it with videos of experts performing the same pose. However, the contours containing key points are insufficient, which leads to a loss of information about body orientations. Chen et al. [2] propose a posture recognition system using Kinect to capture the body map of the practitioner, in which a star like skeleton describes the human body. Some approaches [19, 20] fall prey to commonly occurring anomalies in practical scenarios such as poor illumination, twisted bodies, clutter, and flowing dresses while estimating the poses. The human skeleton is an essential element of human posture detection. Techniques utilizing this often perform distance transformation or thinning, but these techniques lead to high sensitivity to noise and a high computational cost [21].

DeepPose, implemented by Toshev et al. [22], is an excellent alternative to the earlier skeletonization approach. It predicts the motion of an individual by using neural network regressors to determine the coordinates of the body joints. Though body components that are not visible are also located, the technique falls prey to the problem of localization. The output of the model also encounters a delay in providing the result, making it an ineffective real-time predictor. Luo et al. [23] presented a motion replication technique (MoRep)- based yoga training system. The interface suit consists of tactors and inertial measurement units (IMUs), which accurately comprehend the motion of the body. However, it may alter the practitioner's performance. Hsieh et al. [24] developed another yoga training system that compares the distance variance between the practitioner's heat map and the traditional posture of an expert yoga trainer. Their proposed method evaluates the practitioner's posture and provides a score, which indicates the correctness of the posture performed by the practitioner. Convolutional neural networks (CNN) have played an immense role in joint detection.

The implementations involve 2D pose estimation for a single person [25, 26], 3D pose estimation for a single person [27, 28], 2D pose detection for multiple people [29, 30], and 3D pose detection for multiple people [31–33]. Dantone et al. [34] propose a novel nonlinear joint regressor for the estimation of 2D human poses from images. In the technique presented by Tian et al. [35], the model captures higher-order spatial relationships for pose estimation. Another approach to capturing the high-order relationships is with an image-dependent pose estimation model predicted via a global classifier [20, 36, 37]. Shotton et al. [38] provide a useful model to predict poses from single-depth images accurately. Mohanty et al. [39] also base their work on images to classify postures, but the model seems unsuitable for deployment in real-time applications.

The scheme of Yadav et al. [40] introduces the utilization of OpenPose [29], an open source library for multi-person key point detection for yoga pose recognition. To this end, their presented scheme uses OpenPose to extract key points from the frames of the yoga pose sequences. In the subsequent step, a hybrid of CNN and long short-term memory (LSTM) models uses the extracted key points for the prediction of yoga poses. The CNN extracts spatial information from the key points, and LSTM models the evaluation of the yoga poses using these spatial features. Despite its excellent performance, their proposed system has several limitations. For instance, the input video fed to the model is expected to be of a specified duration, which could limit the number of frames in the model. Furthermore, OpenPose fails in the case of overlapping body parts and makes negative predictions on non-human body parts. Also, OpenPose key point detection and prediction by their proposed model takes a considerable amount of time.

2.1.2 ACTIVITY RECOGNITION

Video-based 2D action recognition is a complex problem because it involves high-level feature extraction and the time dimension [45]. In recent years, deep-learning based methods have received more and more attention because of their strong feature processing abilities. The convolution operation is one of the basic parts of deep learning networks for the action recognition task. Karpathy et al. [34] proposed a single-frame action recognition architecture. This method can utilize 2D CNN models which are pre trained on other datasets. However, temporal information is significant in the action recognition task. Some 2D CNN based papers added a time-distributed layer to get temporal information in the videos like paper [44].

To make use of temporal information, researchers found many solutions. 3D CNN [31] is an intuitive way to acquire temporal information from videos. Tran et al. [70] introduced an advanced version of 3D CNN called C3D. They found a better kernel size for 3D CNN and proved their architecture has better performance. Moreover, researchers improved C3D and proposed Residual CNN which is two times faster and smaller with comparative performance [69]. In paper [75], they built an asymmetric 3D convolution depth model which further improves efficiency and effectiveness.

Some works also focus on utilizing pre-trained 2D CNN based models while taking temporal information into consideration [9, 29]. Paper [9] introduced a new 3D CNN architecture called I3D (Two-Stream Inflated 3D CNN) which is based on 2D CNN inflation. Their method has the advantage of using the parameters from 2D CNNs trained on ImageNet [7] by concatenating inflated filters and kernels from existing 2D models. Paper [29] converted pre-trained filters of 2D CNN to a 3D structure without prepossessing, and their parallel 3D CNN architecture remains competitive. RNN (Recurrent Neural Network) and LSTM (Long Short-Term Memory) are also widely used in action recognition tasks [56, 21]. RNN is a recurrent network by performing the same function on each input data. The output of the current stage not only depends on the present input data, but also on the previous stage. LSTM is a better version of RNN which makes it easier to remember past data.

Another way for action recognition is using multi-streams [6]. These methods usually apply several CNNs to make the best use of appearance and motion information. One representative article is [61]. Its model includes two streams: Spatial stream CNN and Temporal Stream CNN. The spatial stream focuses on getting static information from still frames while the Temporal Stream CNN obtains motion information by optical flow images. One of the main problems is that this network lacks information change between these two streams. Paper [22] worked on this limitation and built a bridge that allows information transfer in the two features.

Despite obtaining the action type directly, many researchers work on action recognition tasks utilizing pose estimation results. For regression-based human pose estimation methods, the joint positions are computed directly. Cheron et al. [11] leveraged informative areas around the human joints of the image. Both RGB and optical flow of these parts are fed into the CNN model to get the action results. Paper [45] utilized the 2D joints coordinates to create a 3D image-like matrix that represents the temporal movement of all the joints. Some researchers [43] also decoded the skeleton information using different colors according to the type of joints. An Encoded Human Pose Image (EHPI) is generated according to the joint type and frame number. Sun et al. [64] fed the joints key points to an embedding model, and their model is effective in view-invariant action recognition.

To make use of the rich information of the heat map which is a byproduct of detection based pose estimation methods, lots of literature created effective methods in leveraging heatmaps. In the paper [13], they colorized the heat maps based on the order of the frames. These maps are temporally aggregated and fed into a classification network. Shah et al. [59] improved this method by reweighing motion information of various joints. Segu et al. [58] applied this idea to the 3D pose estimation and action recognition field. Liu et al. [40] accumulated the heatmaps to create two images, which describe the temporal difference of torso shape and pose locations. The two features are fused, and a CNN model is applied to get the classification result. These works got good results but they all need complicated processing on the heatmaps like colorization. In paper [41], researchers made use of two features derived from pose estimation maps: DPI and DTI. This method is straightforward and intuitive without complex processing procedures. What's more, DTI alone contains both joint movement information and body shape information which we found can help other tasks like human exercise counting.

2.1.3 REPETITIVE COUNTING

Repetitive Counting is an important task in the Computer Vision field. Many works on repetitive counting commonly transform the motion to a one-dimensional signal. Frequency information is extracted by signal processing methods like Fourier Transform [20, 52, 15, 39, 4, 50, 3], peak detection [56, 63] or singular value decomposition [12, 51]. These methods assume the motion is periodic and stationary, which is unsuitable in many non-stationary situations. Therefore, Paper [53] replaced Fourier Transform with Wavelet Transform. To handle camera movement and diversity in motion repetitions, they constructed a series of time-varying flow-based signals, which are calculated in the motion foreground segmentation. However, this method failed to take context information into consideration.

The periodic detection problem can also be treated as a problem of finding commonalities between two video sequences [15, 49]. In the paper

[14], the researchers represented the video sequences as histogram-form features, and leveraged a Branch and Bound (R&B) algorithm to find the common events in two videos. Shariat et al. [60] proposed an advanced segmental alignment model which can find the segmental boundaries of common events and pair them automatically. Their methods have better noise immunity when matching sequences. In [49], the researchers proposed a symmetric matrix composed of two action sequences' pairwise difference. A highly efficient graph-based algorithm MUCOS and SMUCOS was proposed for this problem. It is reliable in the unsupervised situations when the semantic content of the videos, the number of periods and the valid duration of the video are unknown. Unlike the former methods, Debidatta et al. [18] introduced a new symmetric matrix. It acts as an intermediate layer to predict the cycle length and valid periodic length. Using this method, it achieved up-to-date accuracy in benchmark QUVA [53].

There are also many other methods that don't fall into the two divisions above. Levy and Wolf [36] employed a CNN model for the whole video to estimate the cycle length. After that, they used two counters to record the number of repetitions so far and the index of the frame in one cycle respectively. The limitation is that cycle length is unchangeable in one video, which is not adaptable for actions with varied frequencies. Topology based method is also an important branch [61, 65]. The ideas are based on approaches from applied topology. They leveraged cohomotopy-based methods to recover the location of object movements by generating a symbolic motion cycle. The created closed curves describe a repeated movement for recurrent animation.

Some researchers also learn from action-recognition tasks [77]. They extracted deep features from BN-Inception Network [30], and transformed the high-dimensional features to a one-dimensional wavelet using PCA (Principal Component Analysis). Signal processing methods are applied to the extracted wavelet to get the counting result. Due to the close relationship between action recognition and counting as both tasks focus on spatial difference throughout the video, many works combine these two tasks together. In the paper [10], they leveraged data from accelerators, and applied classical methods such as naive Bayes classifier, hidden Markov models and peak detection. They achieved over 90 percent accuracy in exercise recognition and the discount rate is about 5 percent. An inertial measurement unit is also used along with the accelerator [57]. They achieved 92% action recognition accuracy and 2.42% miscounting results in 16 gym exercises. Smart phones and smart watches are also widely used in this task, and they obtained better results due to the improvements of algorithms and built-in sensors [24, 63]. Though these methods achieved good accuracy, they cannot be widely applied due to hardware limitations.

Wi-Fi-signals are also used in this multitask. Xiwen et al. [42] proposed a CSI (Channel State Information) based method. Peak-finding algorithms are applied to count repetitive actions, and action type is recognized using KNN (K-Nearest Neighbors) classifier. Even though the Wi-Fi-based method is free of wearing devices, submitting and receiving devices are still necessary. Finally, to the best of our knowledge, papers [1, 35] are the most related works as my thesis, which combine three tasks together. Alatiah et al. [1] generated a new dataset by augmenting UCF101 dataset [62]. OpenPose [7] was applied to estimate 3D human pose. The estimated key points are fed into a CNN model to derive the action class. For the counting task, parameters including major joints and type of motion are preselected. The major joints' angles of specific exercise are calculated from joint positions. The counting result and the correctness of the exercise are determined by the angle-time plot. This work proposes a reliable real-time system. However, exercise type and respective main joints should be set before counting.

Khurana et al. [35] collected exercise videos from gym cameras. They obtained key points utilizing Wang et al.'s [65] method. The key points are gathered to form motion trajectories. Different from this thesis, their method works in the multiple-people situation. Therefore, the trajectories are processed and clustered. The processed features are fed into a multi-layer classifier and a multi-layer regressor to achieve exercise category and counting results respectively. This paper has the advantage of working for multiple persons. However, its accuracy is limited and needs further improvement.

2.1.4 TOP-DOWN VS. BOTTOM-UP APPROACH

Two popular approaches to multi-pose estimation using deep neural networks are top down [25, 26, 27, 28, 29] and bottom-up [11, 30, 31, 32, 33]. The top-down approach essentially bottles down to performing object detection to find a bounding box containing a person in an image, followed by estimating the pose in each of these boxes. While being a viable solution, it suffers from poor performance due to the need of running pose estimation for every person found in the image. The performance is directly correlated with the number of people in the scene, thus lowering the systems performance. Also, if the object detection step fails, it will run bad results through the pipeline. Since top-down approaches make use of an object detector, one can choose a huge variety of existing object detection models such as YOLOv3 [34] and SSD [35] or create a new one such as HRNet [27]. This makes the top-down approach flexible by letting developers tune the speed and accuracy of their pose estimation models to their needs. The other approach, bottom-up, consists of identifying and localizing all the key points in an image and then connecting them into the individual. Starting with the smallest cases and combining them into a general representation of the human pose.

The most recent works in single-stage pose estimation approaches [37], [38] either use depth images directly for inference, or first discretize the generated point clouds into voxels and then estimate a pose in 3D world coordinates. Presently, the Deep-Depth Pose algorithm [37] claims to have the best results among two stage approaches on the synthetic dataset UBC3V. The authors have provided trained models for inference on a dataset called ITOP [47], where they achieve a 100 % accuracy at 10 cm. The primary idea stated is given a depth image, it is possible to directly regress 3D joint coordinates of a human in 3D world space. Trained models for inference on UBC 3V were not provided, so an implementation of this approach, as described below was attempted.

Numerous approaches for 3D estimation of poses from 2D images follow a pattern, often termed as library-based matching. They would first infer 2D poses from the image, and with inverse projection, multiple 3D poses are proposed. These 3D candidates are then compared with all the existing 3D poses in the library mentioned above. This idea forms an inspiration for our DDP approach. Here instead of a full-fledged library, a small collection of poses is obtained. But this is not selected from a library of actual 3D poses. Instead, all the poses in existing training data are clustered, and these cluster centroids serve as bases for a high-dimensional vector space. These bases are also termed as 'prototypes' in the original paper.

2.1.5 ENCODER-DECODER ARCHITECTURE

Most deep learning architecture for 2D human pose estimation starts with an encoder that uses RGB images as input and extracts features using multiple convolutions. Some neural network models, such as mask-RCNN [25], use an encode-decoder architecture, where the output from the encoder is directly fed into a decoder. Which then produces a heat map that represents the probability of where the key points may be located. The exact key points may then be located by selecting the key points from the heat map with the highest likelihood of being the correct one. The downside to this approach is that it may result in a low-resolution output, which in turn is used to create the high-resolution representational keypoints [27]. Using higher resolution images as input may alleviate the problem, but will hurt the performance.

Despite obtaining the action type directly, many researchers work on action recognition tasks utilizing pose estimation results. For regression-based human pose estimation methods, the joints positions are computed directly. Cheron et al. [11] leveraged informative areas around the human joints of the image. Both RGB and optical flow of these parts are fed into the CNN model to get the action results. Paper [45] utilized the 2D joints coordinates to create a 3D image-like matrix that represents the temporal movement of all the joints. Some researchers [43] also decoded the skeleton information using different colour according to the type of joints. An Encoded Human Pose Image (EHPI) is generated according to the joint type and frame number. Sun et al. [64] fed the joints keypoints to an embedding model, and their model is effective in view-invariant action recognition.

2.1.6 DATASETS AND KEYPOINTS

There exist several datasets that are used in training and evaluation of human pose estimation systems. Some of them vary in terms of number of keypoints and what they correspond to in the human body. This section will briefly mention a few important datasets. COCO [36], short for Common objects in context, is a large dataset of labeled objects, first presented in a paper in 2014 and used to aid computer recognition systems in training and testing. The dataset has been an important driver for evaluating computer vision systems and a motivating base for competition among professionals and hobbyists. The researchers proposed that in order to build systems that solve computer vision tasks and be effective out in the wild, the training images needed to represent a diverse background context.

One major flaw with the COCO human keypoint dataset, is that it lacks sufficient key points for the feet. Without foot coordinates, it is hard to say how the subjects interact with the floor. An estimation has to be made in the case of collision detection with the floor or other applications have to be applied, which are often prone to errors. With the release of OpenPose, they included annotated foot keypoints, which were a subset of the COCO dataset, consisting of 14K images from the training set and 545 images from the validation set. This led to a total of 25 key points produced by OpenPose and has shown to improve the overall performance of the system.

Instead of detecting key points that correspond to human limbs, a research team presented a study in 2018 [37], along with their dense pose estimation system, a dataset of annotated pixels that correspond to the 3D surface of that individual. This dataset consists of 50K COCO images that are manually annotated to describe the image-to-surface data. The dataset enables a more accurate mapping of RGB pixels to a semantic 3D object representation. Until 2017, most pose estimation dataset did not include tracking of multiple people over video. This made it hard to evaluate the tracking capabilities of human pose estimation systems. In a paper published in 2017 a dataset named PoseTrack [38] was proposed that contained over 150,000 annotated poses including tracking. By using the VATIC Tool [39] the research team was able to effectively annotate a total of 15 key points for each visible individual in each image.

Low-cost depth sensors have had an enormous impact on consumer markets (like Microsoft XBOX) as well as multiple robotics applications like on drones for indoor/outdoor navigation, etc. Just like their monocular counterpart, depth-based 3D Pose estimation techniques can also be classified as either Two-Stage or Single-Stage. Shotton and Girshick [32] used Random Forests to classify each pixel into body parts, and subsequently derived joint locations from these maps with a Mean-Shift based approach.

Other two-stage approaches like [33] use depth map labels combined with probabilistic graphical models for final inference involving graph cuts. Modern deep-learning approaches like [34] first segment depth maps using CNNs, and then reconstruct segmented point-clouds to obtain 3D joint locations. A library of 3D poses is also used in some approaches for fitting into the outputs of a segmented depth map, instead of directly regressing, as in [35]. Although this approach claims to observe exceptionally good results, it still fails in cases where poses are unexpectedly different at test time.

Very few works in the literature have demonstrated use of semi-automatic annotation policies on limited datasets like [39], [40]. Some other works like [34], [37] use synthetic and real datasets individually to benchmark their algorithms. A lot of studies in recent literature [41], [42], [43] show that using synthetic datasets while training can boost the learning performance. But a controlled study on what impact these techniques could have in improving human pose estimation on real datasets cannot be found in existing literature.

Also, a very recent development in 3D computer vision known as PointNets [44] has revolutionized multiple recognition and detection tasks in 3D in a space-efficient and rotation-invariant manner. Therefore, a new single-stage neural network architecture inspired from PointNets is proposed to estimate 3D joint coordinates from depth data. Another key contribution of this work would be to understand the impacts of combining real and synthetic datasets in improving human pose estimation on real human datasets.

2.2 REAL TIME SURVEY

Many commercial solutions exist in the market for interactive at-home exercise, such as Peloton ($2000), Tonal ($3000), and MIRROR ($1500). However, none offer real-time feedback, except for Mirror, which charges an additional $40 per session with a live trainer. Furthermore, none of these are specifically designed to address free weights. The proliferation of machine learning research in the past decade has also trickled into exercise science. A number of researchers have attempted to build models to address the problems associated with exercise classification and form detection. One example is Gym Cam, a tool for detecting, recognizing, and tracking simultaneous exercises in unconstrained scenes. The researchers used an approach that they call "frequency-based feature matching," which uses human pose estimation to track joint movements, surveying for periodic movements, and identifying individual exercises based on joint trajectory and frequency sampling within those localities [14].

Another application is Pose Trainer, a tool for correcting exercise posture with pose estimation, evaluating form based on angles and distances between joints, and using thresholding to determine improper movement patterns. While Pose Trainer's function is remarkably similar to what we are trying to accomplish, it focuses on minor bodily tendencies for more niche exercises like the bicep curl and the shoulder shrug. These are known as isolation exercises, and unlike compound movements (such as the big three), they only involve a single joint. The risk of injury from performing these isolation movements is quite small. Focusing on isolation exercises allows the pose trainer to focus on the movement of a single joint, making angle and position analysis a relatively straightforward task [15].

Among other physical activities, powerlifting is one of the most popular directions in fitness. Squatting is the basic exercise performed by athletes.

Being simple at first glance, this exercise is often not performed correctly due to the heavy weight of the barbell, which is why many athletes need a personal trainer. When training human pose estimation models for fitness apps, it is required to consider that men and women's bodies are physiologically different. If the model was trained only on men's images, it will return accurate results for only male users but not for females. Since the difference in men's and women's body postures during physical training is very big, the model may output incorrect results even if the exercise was performed correctly. Thus, it's important to consider this aspect when developing a fitness app based on human pose estimation.

It's important to understand that the human pose estimation model will analyze the user's body based on those images of people used for training. Thereby, the model's perception of the user's body will be based on people's bodies from the training images. There is no guarantee that the training dataset included images with a similar body structure. The exercise estimation involves the detection of the exercise start and end, where the fitness app is expected to analyze the exercise duration period directly. In squatting with a barrel, the app can analyze the positions of the user's hands and shoulders by using arbitrary hard coded thresholds. The error may occur when the arm angles briefly go above the arbitrary threshold.

The comparison of movements between two people is one more technique to estimate the correctness of exercise performance. The data are taken as frames from two video records: the reference video with the correct exercise technique and the input video of a user who utilizes a fitness app to analyze the exercise's performance. In order to compare these two videos, it is necessary to identify the position of 3D key points on both videos, align them, and measure distances between the user's joints and joints of an athlete from the reference video. The problem lies in unusual movements and limitations of existing datasets. When the human pose estimation model processes frames with a strictly frontal view, the quality of results may be low. It is because the datasets used for training human pose estimation models still do not contain enough images of movements, poses, and different perspectives.

Squatting is not a single exercise where AI-based fitness apps may return errors. One more example is kicking using legs in martial arts. When a person does a quick kick with the leg, the deep learning model might not catch this movement. The reason for that might be the fast transition of the leg, which can be partially caused by the blurring of leg key points.

One more reason is that the 2D key point dataset (COCO in our case) may not contain such kind of limb images, thereby, 3D predictions for the lower part of the body does not reflect real movements since the 2D detections that are used as an input for 3D pose prediction were detected incorrectly.

Push-ups may also be a challenge for the human pose estimation model. When detecting 2D key points of arms and legs from the video of the athlete performing push-ups, the model returns a significant number of errors. We decided to check whether it would work properly if we rotate the video so that we could analyze the athlete's movements from the vertical position, and it worked well. This issue proved our assumption about the insufficiency of visual data in the open datasets once again.

Our approach is more holistic. Instead of focusing on one or two specific joints, we attempt to evaluate the position of multiple joints in relation to each other to provide feedback based on the type of exercise the user is performing. We use our Human Pose Estimation model to track these joints and discover relationships between them based on known bad form tendencies. If certain joints are positioned at the wrong angle or at the wrong distance from each other, the chances of long-term injury can be quite severe. By identifying these high-level form breakdowns that beginner lifters often neglect, we can mitigate potential future injuries.

CHAPTER THREE

METHODOLOGY

3.1 PROPOSED MODEL

The system as a whole takes an exercise video from the user as input and outputs a table of detected technique issues for the given video. However, before the final result is presented to the user, the data has to be processed by multiple components within the system. The input video is first passed on to the Pose Extraction System where it is processed by either OpenPose, AlphaPose or WrnchAI. For this thesis each video is run through all of the systems to compare their individual ability to detect technique issues in workout training. The data from the unique human pose estimation systems are then processed and passed on to the document database.

Then the Action Recognition System extracts the key points from the database and runs them through the MobileNet classification neural models to detect the performed exercise and filming angle. The exercise is classified by using dynamic time warping along with the MobileNet neural network. The result of the classification is then stored back to the document database with a reference to the related key point dataset. Lastly the Technique Evaluation System retrieves all related data from the database and runs specific vector calculations based on the predicted exercise and detection angle. The resulting technique analysis is then stored in the database and is ready to be presented to the user along with the detected exercise and filming angle. An overview of the full system architecture is shown in Figure 3.1.

The input to this part of the system is a raw unprocessed and unfiltered exercise video. The exercise video is first processed by the implemented human pose estimation systems OpenPose. The resulting dataset is then stripped of unnecessary data, transformed to a universal format and filtered for inaccurate estimations. The resulting key points are then indexed and stored in the database.

The Action Recognition system starts by extracting all processed key points from the document database. Further each key point is processed as a time series to detect both the filming angle and the performed exercise. Data normalization and noise filtering is applied, before the filming angle and exercise detection are performed separately. Then it selects a subset of relevant vector formulas based on the predicted exercise and filming angle. All selected vector formulas are then calculated to detect if any technique issues are present in the given pose estimation dataset. The output is a list containing all detected technique issues for the dataset. If none are detected, an empty list is returned.

In the MobileNet model, convolutional lyers act as a feature extractor and are specifically used to extract some useful information by understanding video data's internal representation while short-term and long-term dependencies can be identified using neural networks. Our proposed model's main idea is to integrate the benefits of various deep learning approaches in an effective manner. MobileNet uses depth-wise separable convolutions as efficient building blocks. Traditional convolutions are often very resource intensive, and depth wise separable convolutions are able to reduce the number of trainable parameters and operations and also speed up convolutions in two steps:

• The first step calculates an intermediate result by convolving on each of the channels independently. This is the depth-wise convolution.

• In the second step, another convolution merges the outputs of the previous step into one. This gets a single result from a single feature at a time, and then is applied to all the filters in the output layer. This is the point-wise convolution, or: Shape of the depth-wise convolution X Number of filters.

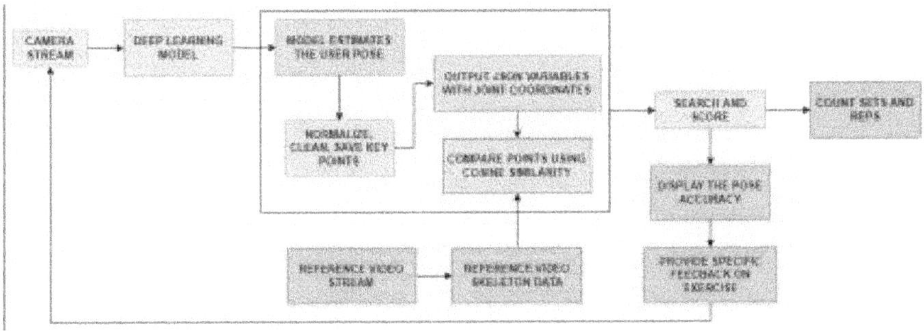

Fig 3.1. Architecture for Estimation of Workout Postures and Feedback Providing System

MobileNet is built on depth-wise separable convolution layers. Each depth-wise separable convolution layer consists of a depth-wise convolution and a pointwise convolution. Counting depth-wise and pointwise convolutions as separate layers, a MobileNet has 28 layers. A standard MobileNet has 4.2 million parameters which can be further reduced by tuning the width multiplier hyperparameter appropriately. The size of the input image is $224 \times 224 \times 3$.

The MobileNet architecture has three defining characteristics:

- Depth wise separable convolutions
- Thin input and output bottlenecks between layers
- Shortcut connections between bottleneck layers

The MobileNet model is based on depth-wise separable convolutions which is a procedure of factorized convolutional which factorizes a regular convolution into a depth-wise convolution and a 1×1 convolution named a pointwise convolution [26]. MobileNet depth-wise convolution uses a single filter to every input channel. The pointwise convolution then applies a 1×1 convolution to merge the outputs with the depth wise convolution. A regular convolution both filters and merges inputs into a new set of outputs in one step. The depth-wise separable convolution splits this into two layers, a separate layer for filtering and a separate layer for merging. This factorization has the effect of extremely reducing computation and model size.

We use a pre-trained model to modify the classifier task so that it's able to recognize workout exercises in the following steps:

- Delete the top layer (the classification layer).
- Add a new classifier layer.
- Train only one layer by freezing the rest of the network.
- A single neuron is enough to solve a binary classification problem.
- Freeze the base model and train the newly-created classifier layer.
- Set base model. Trainable = False to avoid changing the weights and train only the new layer.

- Set training in base model to False to avoid keeping track of statistics in the batch norm layer.

The MobileNet structure is built on depth wise separable convolutions as mentioned in the previous section except for the first layer which is a full convolution. By defining the network in such simple terms, you are able to easily explore network structure to find a good network. All layers in MobileNet are followed by a batch norm and ReLU nonlinearity with the exception of the final fully connected layer which has no nonlinearity and feeds into a SoftMax layer for classification. Figure 3.2 contrasts a layer with regular convolutions, batch norm and ReLU non-linearity to the factorized layer with depth wise convolution, 1×1 pointwise convolution as well as batch norm and ReLU after each convolutional layer. Down sampling is handled with stride convolution in the depth wise convolutions as well as in the first layer. A final average pooling reduces the spatial resolution to 1 before the fully connected layer. Counting depth wise and pointwise convolutions as separate layers, MobileNet has 28 layers.

Instance formless light matrix operations are not typically faster than thick matrix operations until a very high level of sparsity. This model structure puts nearly all of the computation into dense 1×1 convolutions. This can be implemented with highly optimized general matrix multiply (GEMM) functions. Often convolutions are implemented by a GEMM but require an initial reordering in memory in order to map it to a GEMM. This method is used in the popular Caffe package. 1×1 convolutions do not require this reordering in memory and can be implemented directly with GEMM which is one of the most improved numerical linear algebra algorithms. MobileNet models were trained in TensorFlow using RMSprop with asynchronous gradient descent. However, opposed to training large models use less regularization and data augmentation techniques that small models rarely have trouble with overfitting. When training MobileNet, use side heads or label smoothing and additionally reduce the number of distortions by limiting the size of small crops that are used in large Inception training. Additionally, we found that it was important to put very little or no weight decay on the depth wise filters since there are so few parameters in them.

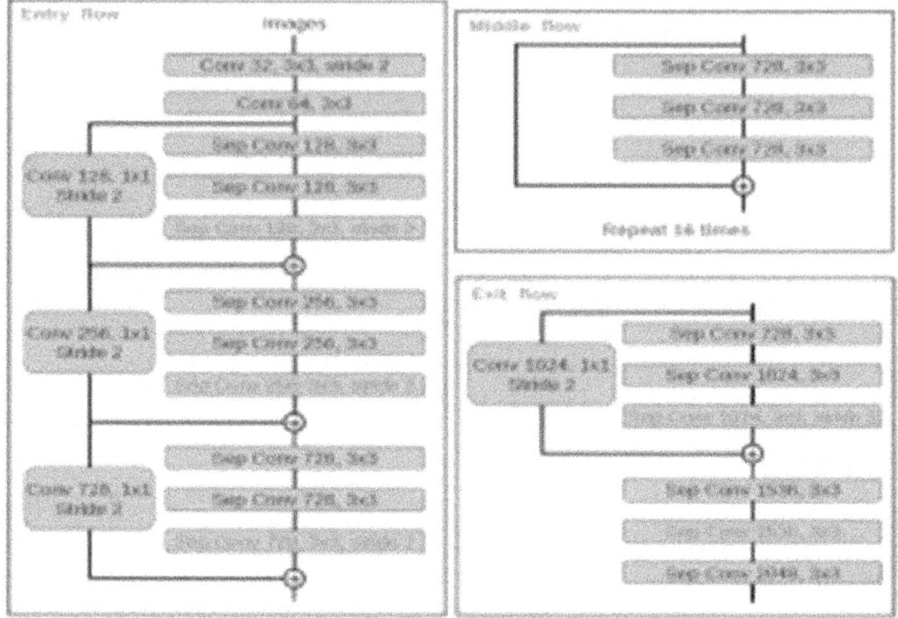

Fig 3.2. Architectural Model for MobileNet

We use Early stopping, a form of regularization used to avoid overfitting on the training dataset. Early stopping keeps track of the validation loss, if the loss stops decreasing for several epochs in a row the training stops. Traditional convolutions are often very resource-intensive, and depth wise separable convolutions are able to reduce the number of trainable parameters and operations and also speed up convolutions. Initially, we calculate an intermediate result by convolving on each of the channels independently. In the second step, another convolution merges the outputs of the previous step into one. This gets a single result from a single feature at a time, and then is applied to all the filters in the output layer.

3.2 WORKOUT POSE ESTIMATION

To be able to answer the research question precisely, the first major decision to be taken was the selection of human pose estimation candidates to be used for the solution. With new candidates presented every year, the options are many and the features to consider even more. Speed, accuracy, body models and availability are all important aspects to consider when picking pose estimation systems. Research into the realm of human pose estimation revealed some clear state-of-the-art candidates. Some being well tested and applied in multiple research and others with less exploration. But all stating to be among the best pose estimation technologies available.

DensePose: Published by Facebook in 2019 and aims at mapping all human pixels from a RGB Image to a 3D model. Unique of its kind and provides opportunities never examined before. Open source.

- OpenPose: Released as an open-source project in 2017. Since then, it has become the most popular human pose estimation library available. Big community, great documentation and well tested.
- HRNet: A recent project released in 2019 that maintains a high-resolution representation and has so far outperformed all existing models on key point detection earlier tested on the COCO dataset.
- WrnchAI: Is the only closed source software on the list. However, third party testing against OpenPose revealed more than 2x faster processing speed, significantly smaller model sizes and lower GPU RAM requirement.
- AlphaPose: open-source software released in 2018 and receiving further development in 2020. Scores remarkably better than OpenPose for several tests on the COCO and MPII datasets.

Fig 3.3. Data Points Detection using OpenPose System

Fig 3.4. Pose Estimation with Annotations using OpenPose System

The input to this part of the system is a raw unprocessed and unfiltered exercise video. The exercise video is first processed by the three implemented human pose estimation systems OpenPose, AlphaPose and WrnchAI. The resulting dataset is then stripped of unnecessary data, transformed to a universal format and filtered for inaccurate estimations. The resulting key points are then indexed and stored in the database. The action recognition system starts by extracting all processed key points from the document database. Further each key point is processed as a time series to detect both the filming angle and the performed exercise. Data normalization and noise filtering is applied, before the filming angle and exercise detection are performed separately. A dynamic time warping algorithm is used to compare similarity between key points and classify each sequence using a MobileNet architecture.

Extracted key points are initially rendered from the Pose Extraction System and stored in the document database. The Action Recognition System then extracts the key points and uses them to predict the angle the key points are filmed from and the exercise they represent. This information is then stored to the document database with a reference to the related dataset already stored. Consequently, the pose estimation system extracts both the key point information from the pose extraction system and the predictions from the action recognition system to evaluate for different technique aspects on the dataset.

CHAPTER FOUR

FORMULATION OF DATA, TOOLS AND PLATFORMS

4.1 DATASET ELICITATIONs

The process of creating a dataset for video generation and action recognition, focusing on fitness exercises. Key requirements were established, such as using four subjects (two male and two female athletes), performing various exercises with different severity levels of technique issues, and ensuring only the exercising athlete is visible in the videos. Standardized equipment was used, and filming angles were specified. The dataset, derived from the Penn Action Dataset, consisted of videos filmed in a gym, with a focus on specific angles and exercise repetitions.

Data preprocessing involved filtering out inaccuracies in human pose estimations, primarily based on confidence scores. Thresholds were set to remove low-confidence estimations and points with high variability. Techniques like translational invariance were applied to ensure consistency in data interpretation. The software requirements for this project included Jupyter Notebook, Windows 11, and various libraries for data processing, machine learning, and visualization, along with APIs like OpenPose, DensePose, and AlphaPose.

4.1.1 PREREQUISITES FOR THE DATASET

Before starting the filming process, it was necessary to create a few rules to set the foundation for the video generation process. The results were the following requirements described more thoroughly later on:

- Four subjects should be used to cover for body variations. Two male and two female athletes.
- Each subject should perform all of the technical aspects listed, for both exercises and filming angle.
- Each subject should do each technique issue at two severity degrees. Moderate and high.
- Each subject should do one correctly performed video of each exercise from each of the specified angles.
- No other person than the athlete doing the exercise should be visible in the video.
- Standard weightlifting bars and weight plates should be used to make the videos as close to reality as possible.
- Subjects should evenly divide lifting in shoes and shoeless to cover for different equipment used.

The first requirement ensures that the model created can detect a wider range of body composition and is not fitted to one specific athlete. A small set of athletes that involves both genders will not cover all possible differences between athletes, but will cover enough variations to give the model some flexibility. Thus, proving that the model can detect cases in the given scope in addition to related cases where the variations are somehow similar. The second requirement gives us a sample set of technique issues to test the proposed vector formulas on. This further helps to cover for variations for each technique aspect by having diverse execution and variation from regular movement patterns.

The third requirement deals with how clearly or excessively the technique issues should be performed when an issue is provoked on purpose. An exercise with a distinct technique issue present would be easier for a system to detect, since it is further from the general movement pattern of an optimal execution. However, movement patterns that are too far away from a correct execution are less likely to occur on a regular basis, and thus will not be as useful to detect for most users. On the other hand, the bigger the deviation from an optimal pattern is, the higher the chances are for a serious injury to occur. For this reason, we adopt two degrees of severity when performing a technique aspect: moderate and high. All athletes also performed a correct movement of each exercise from the two specified angles. This is to generate a subset of correctly performed exercises that can be evaluated on the same basis as the rest of the videos. The main purpose of this is to disclose false positives resulting from inaccurate vector calculations. As well as having a base set for reference, that should not report for any technique issues by the system.

Another prerequisite for the video generation was that the only person visible in the frame should be the one performing the exercise. This choice is not due to possibility but rather simplicity, since all the selected pose estimation systems have multi-person detection. However, ensuring that only one person is visible makes the data processing easier as well as making the pose estimation faster and the resulting dataset smaller. The last requirement deals with the equipment used by the athlete during the video generation. Making sure to use standardized bars and weight lifting plates provide videos with the same equipment found in most training centers. The standardized weight lifting plates are also of such size that they cover some parts of the subject performing the exercise. It is important to see how the human pose estimation systems respond and behave under these circumstances, since most athletes perform these exercises using weighted barbells. The footwear requirement is simply to test if different footwear result in a different outcome from the pose estimation. This is important because athletes perform exercises with everything from lifting shoes to barefoot.

4.1.2 DATA COLLECTION

Penn Action Dataset (University of Pennsylvania) contains 2326 images/video sequences of 10 different actions and human joint annotations for each sequence. The filming process itself was performed at a regular crowded gym with a standard mobile phone camera so that the preconditions would be the same as for possible end users. A big focus point for the filming was to hit the desired angles as close as possible and to hold the camera steady to avoid too much inaccuracy due to camera movement. The two angles to be used during filming were taken from a front and a side view. Together this covers all technique issues and are described below:

- The Front View: Is straight in front of the subject with the athlete in the center of the screen. The whole person should be visible with some space on all edges for good measure.
- The Side View: This is on the right side of the subject and the whole athlete should be visible at the center of the screen. The angle should be such that the right side of the athlete's body covers the left side.

Each video clip is a short snippet where the subject performs the given exercise with or without some technique aspect present from one angle at a time. The video clip begins with the user in the starting position and ends when the athlete is back at the starting position after performing one repetition of the exercise. As mentioned earlier each technique aspect was filmed twice, with two degrees of severity; moderate and high. This choice was made to test the solution on different clarity to see to what extent it would be able to detect errors performed by the subjects.

Specifications

- Length: Videos ranging from 4 seconds to 10 seconds in length.
- Quality: The videos were filmed in either 4k with 60 frames per second or in 1080x1920 pixels with 30 frames per second. All raw, unprocessed, and unfiltered.
- Size: The size of the videos is between 53 megabytes and 9 megabytes.

4.2 DATASET PREPROCESSING AND FILTERING

The final and considerably most important data processing task to be performed on the material was the data filtering. This process filters away data points with low probability to be accurate. This is done by removing points expected to be inaccurate by the human pose estimation systems itself as well as filter away trailing points with unnatural high variability. This process is absolutely crucial for the accuracy of the solution. By removing probable inaccurate estimated points, the chance of detecting technique issues that do not exist decreases as well. Thus, being one of the most important steps to avoid false positives.

All the three human pose estimation systems provide a confidence score of how likely each estimation is to be correct along with the data points. The simplest and most effective way of filtering to remove inaccurate estimations was to disregard key points with a low confidence score. Since the videos are captured in a controlled environment with only one person visible in the center of the screen, they are more likely to estimate well. But to safeguard against completely wrong estimates especially from the side view, a confidence score threshold was decided on.

All confidence scores with lower than 70% probability were discarded and not used in the final solution for the action recognition and technique evaluation tasks. The choice of 70% was to make sure most key points would pass through the filter but at the same time filter away some estimated points with insecurity. The dataset contains key points for every frame of the video and is therefore detailed enough to detect technique aspects even if key points for some frames are disregarded.

However, all rules have exceptions. Some calculations required a confidence score threshold up to 90% due to noise that might cause false positives and were therefore adjusted accordingly. The side view key points had a significantly lower confidence score average than the rest of the data. For this reason, it was necessary to lower the confidence score threshold down to 60% for all videos produced with a filming angle from the side.

Due to innate inaccuracies in human pose estimation systems and computer vision systems in general it is necessary to filter out key points that scored high on probability but had too great of a distance difference from the previous frame. These inaccuracies may occur due to noise in filming or other distortions and may trigger a false positive in our results. To avoid this inaccurate data, we filter out the key points that highly deviate from points close to itself. The data is formatted into a dictionary where the key is the key point name, and the value contains the x coordinate, y coordinate or the probability of it being true. The index of this array is treated as our frame and if a value is missing it is filled in as a null.

- x: X coordinate normalized to the range $[0,1]$
- y: Y coordinate normalized to the range $[0,1]$
- z: Confidence score in the range $[0,1]$

The key points retrieved from the human pose estimation systems were normalized image coordinates. This means that the key points are dependent on the subject's position relative to the camera. To account for this problem, we had to achieve translational invariance before passing the data on to the classifier. The way this was achieved was to make the neck key point center of the coordinate system. This was done by subtracting the neck (x,y) pair from all other key point coordinates in the dataset. For data models that did not contain a neck key point, the center point of the shoulders was simply used instead.

An optimal solution would also try to achieve scale invariance. However, this would require making the distance between the left and the right shoulder 1 by dividing all other key points by this distance. But the distance between the shoulders is not the actual distance but rather a 2D projection onto the image plane. This makes it prone to failures when the subject's body is not facing directly towards the front of the camera as with the side view detection. For this reason, it was not possible to achieve scale invariance for all data in the dataset. The benefit of using the shoulders on a front viewing angle is that the shoulder distance remains relatively constant throughout the videos.

4.3 SOFTWARE REQUIREMENT

- IDE / FRAMEWORK: Jupyter Notebook
- OPERATING SYSTEM: Windows 11
- LIBRARIES: Pandas, NumPy, OpenCV, Random, JSON, IO, Scikit-Learn, Keras, TensorFlow, Matplotlib, Tkinter
- DESIGNING TOOL: DRAW.IO
- SERVER-SIDE TECHNOLOGY: Python Programming
- APPLICATION PROGRAMMING INTERFACE: OpenPose API, DensePose API, AlphaPose API

1. IDE / FRAMEWORK

- Jupyter Notebook:

JupyterLab is the latest web-based interactive development environment for notebooks, code, and data. Its flexible interface allows users to configure and arrange work flows in data science, scientific computing, computational journalism, and machine learning.

2. LIBRARIES
This project can be implemented by using various technologies like:

- OpenCV:

OpenCV is an open-source Python library, which is used to understand the content of the digital image. The CV is the abbreviation form of computer vision. It extracts the description from the real-time image or digital image and performs many tasks such as face detection, face recognition, blob detection, edge-detection, image filter, template matching, and etc.

- NumPy:

NumPy is a library for the Python programming language, adding support for large, multi dimensional arrays and matrices, along with a large collection of high-level mathematical functions to operate on these arrays.

- Pandas:

Pandas is a software library written for the Python programming language for data manipulation and analysis. In particular, it offers data structures and operations for manipulating numerical tables and time series.

- Matplotlib:

Matplotlib is a plotting library for the Python programming language and its numerical mathematics extension NumPy. It provides an object-oriented API for embedding plots into applications using general-purpose GUI toolkits.

- SciKit-Learn:

Scikit-learn is a free software machine learning library for the Python programming language. It features various classification, regression and clustering algorithms.

- TensorFlow:

TensorFlow is a free and open-source software library for machine learning and artificial intelligence. It can be used across a range of tasks but has a particular focus on training and inference of deep neural networks.

- Keras:

Keras is an open-source software library that provides a Python interface for artificial neural networks. Keras acts as an interface for the TensorFlow library.

- OpenPose API:

OpenPose has represented the first real-time multi-person system to jointly detect human body, hand, facial, and foot key points (in total 135 key points) on single images.

- MediaPipe:

MediaPipe offers cross-platform, customizable ML solutions for live and streaming media.

- PIL:

PIL is the Python Imaging Library which provides the python interpreter with image editing capabilities. PIL.Image.new () method creates a new image with the given mode and size. Size is given as a (width, height)-tuple, in pixels.

- Random:

The random module is another library of functions that can extend the basic features of python. Other modules we have seen so far are string, math, time and graphics. With the exception of the graphics module, all of these modules are built into python.

- JSON:

JSON is a syntax for storing and exchanging data. JSON is text, written with JavaScript object notation. Python has a built-in package called JSON, which can be used to work with JSON data.

- IO:

The IO module provides Python's main facilities for dealing with various types of I/O. There are three main types of I/O: text I/O, binary I/O and raw I/O. These are generic categories, and various backing stores can be used for each of them. A Concrete object belonging to any of these categories is called a file object.

3. DESIGNING TOOL

- DRAW. IO:

Diagrams.net is a free and open-source cross-platform graph drawing software developed in HTML5 and JavaScript. Its interface can be used to create diagrams such as flowcharts, wireframes, UML diagrams, organizational charts, and network diagrams.

4. SERVER-SIDE TECHNOLOGY

- PYTHON:

Python is a high-level, general-purpose and a very popular programming language. Python programming language (latest Python 3) is being used in web development, Machine Learning applications, along with all cutting-edge technology in the Software Industry. Python Programming Language is very well suited for Beginners, also for experienced programmers with other programming languages like C++ and Java.

Features of Python:

- Easy to code
- Free and Open Source
- Object-Oriented Language
- High-Level Language
- Dynamically Typed Language
- Interpreted Language

4.4 HARDWARE REQUIREMENT

- PROCESSOR: Core i5
- HARD DISK: Minimum 256 GB
- RAM: Minimum 4 GB
- GRAPHICS CARD: NVIDIA GEFORCE GTX (4 GB)

CHAPTER FIVE

DESIGN AND IMPLEMENTATION

5.1 SYSTEM DESIGN

In this chapter, a three-stage CNN-based framework is proposed for 2D pose estimation for a single person in RGB videos. The convolutional network is widely used in pose estimation and other image-processing tasks. In this thesis, the task of 2D pose estimation of a single person in an RGB video is broken down into three sub-tasks: human detection, 2D pose estimation, and workout classification. To each sub-task, an independent module has been applied to solve the problem and provides output to the following module. Figure 5.1 shows the pipeline of the proposed method.

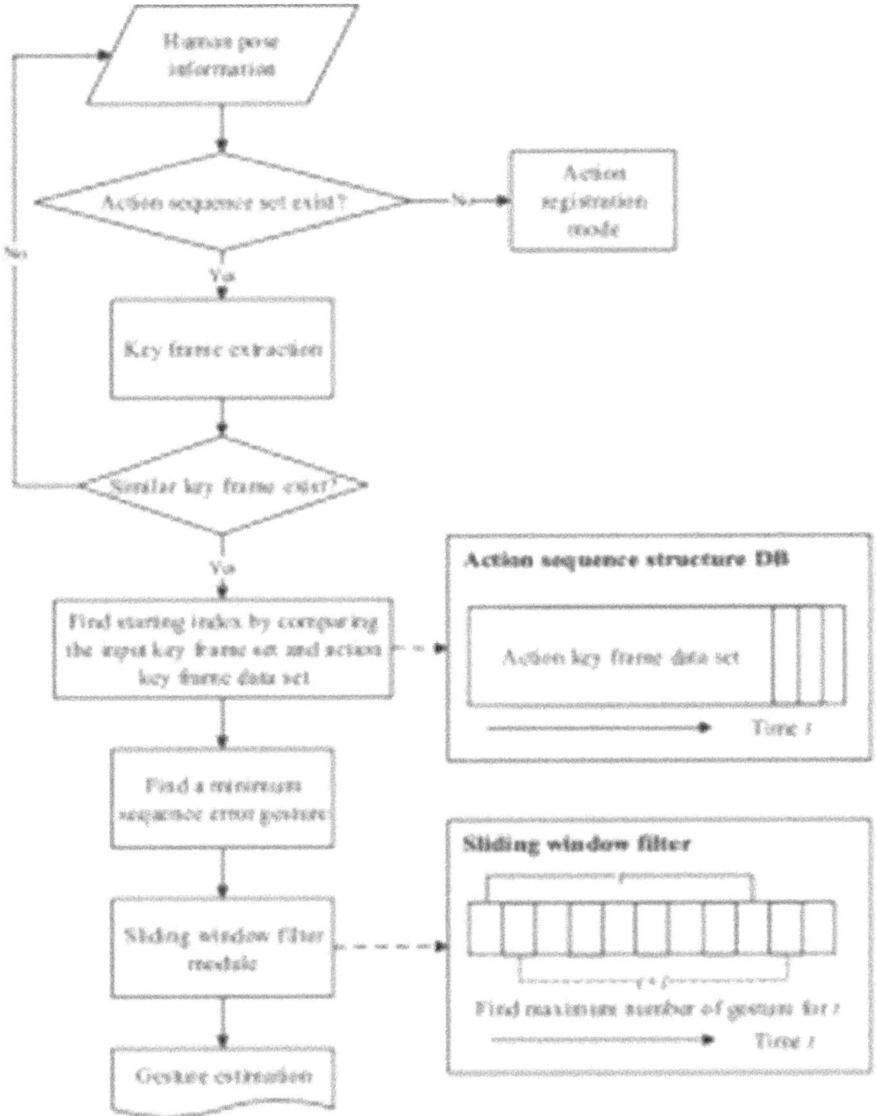

Fig 5.1 Architectural Flow for Workout Postures and Feedback Providing System

The system as a whole accepts a user-supplied workout video as input and generates a table of identified technical problems for the supplied video.

The data must first be processed by a number of system components before the user is shown the final output. The input video is initially sent to the Pose Extraction System, where OpenPose, AlphaPose, or WrnchAI process it. For the purpose of this thesis, each video is put through each system to compare how well they can each identify technique problems during exercise. After processing, the data from the distinct human pose estimation systems is sent to the document database.

The Action Recognition System then pulls the crucial information from the database and feeds it into the MobileNet classification neural models to identify the workout that was completed and the camera angle. Using the MobileNet neural network and dynamic temporal warping, the exercise is categorized. The categorization outcome is then referenced in the document database together with the relevant key point dataset. Finally, based on the anticipated workout and detection angle, the Technique Evaluation System downloads all pertinent data from the database and performs specialized vector calculations. The technique analysis that results is then saved in the database and is prepared to be shown to the user along with the exercise that was detected and the filming angle.

This system's input is a raw, unedited, and unfiltered fitness video. First, the workout footage is analyzed by OpenPose, a human posture estimate algorithm. The resulting dataset is then purified of extraneous information, converted to a common format, and checked for inaccurate estimates. The key points that are produced are then indexed and kept in the database.

The Action Recognition system begins by removing all significant points from the document database that have been processed. Additionally, each key point is analyzed as a time series to identify the exercise that was completed and the camera angle. Prior to doing the exercise detection and filming angle detection individually, data normalization and noise filtering are undertaken. Then, based on the anticipated workout and shooting angle, a selection of pertinent vector formula is chosen. To determine if there are any methodological problems in the provided pose estimation dataset, all selected vector formula is then computed. The result is a list of all technique flaws found in the dataset. An empty list is returned if none were discovered.

5.2 SEQUENCE DIAGRAM

The training phase is the phase of the process in which the classifier is built. In this phase, we recognize some poses. Completing the pose estimation phase concludes that a classifier is built and it can be used in the classifying phase. Figure 5.2 depicts the temporal sequence of the training phase showing the collaboration among all the modules that participate in it. Summarized, the training phase occurs in the following sequence. First, the system needs to detect what kind of activity the user is performing. If what he is saying is a valid pose, then it will be labeled and sent to a node in charge of communicating the interaction modules. The extracted key point labels arrive at the deep learning module which will gather the label describing the human pose and the data from the camera module. The pose_trainer node is the node which fuses the information of the skeleton model and the labels told by the user. The pose_classifier node processes the skeleton messages using the learnt model and sends the output to the voice system.

1. Position Semantics

(a) SIT: Defines that the user is sitting.

(b) STAND: Defines that the user is standing.

2. Action Semantics

(a) TURNED: Defines that the user is turned.

(b) LOOKING: Defines that the user is standing.

3. Direction Semantics

(a) LEFT: Defines that the action that is doing the user is towards his own left side. For example, if it is pointing, it is doing to her left.

(b) FORWARD: Defines that the action performed by the user is towards her front. (c) RIGHT: Defines that the action performed by the user is towards her right

CHAPTER SIX

RESULT AND DISCUSSION

6.1 DATASET QUALITY ASSESSMENT

This section will present the data analyzing methods used on the output data to evaluate the systems data quality. Here we will look at both quantitative and qualitative methods to analyze the data quality. The quantitative methods involve calculating precision and recall to measure percentage of correct estimations as well as percentage of technique issues actually found by the system. The qualitative analyses engage in talks with an expert to ensure the technique aspect in the video foundation is correct and to compare the findings with a qualitative review of the same videos. At the end of the section, the evaluation dataset used for the quantitative data assessment will be presented.

6.1.1 QUANTITATIVE DATA ANALYSIS

The quantitative data analysis will be the main quality assessment activity for evaluating the system's overall ability to correctly identify technique issues related to risk of injury. Here we define a true technique issue (ground truth) to be the one we have categorized in our videos. The formulas calculated here are based on the videos of the subjects created in this thesis. The performance of the networks is evaluated based on the classification accuracy, precision, specificity, and sensitivity throughout the experimentation. As determined by counting the number of correct predictions to the total number of predictions, classification accuracy is defined as:

44

$$\text{Accuracy} = \frac{TP + TN}{TP + TN + FP + FN} \qquad (1)$$

where, TP = True Positive, FP = False Positive, TN = True Negative, FN = False Negative.

Precision is a mathematical computation that analyzes the number of valid true positives to the true positives predictions and can be calculated as follows:

$$\text{Precision} = \frac{TP}{TP + FP} \qquad (2)$$

The true positive rate is obtained by calculating sensitivity, which is the percentage of true positive cases that is perfectly classified according to its class. The sensitivity can be mathematically written as:

$$\text{Sensitivity} = \frac{TP}{TP + FN} \qquad (3)$$

We also assess specificity by computing true negative values, which measure the percentage of true negative cases that is correctly categorized as based on its class as shown by:

$$\text{Specificity} = \frac{TN}{TN + FP} \qquad (4)$$

For this solution, a true positive would mean that the system has correctly predicted a technique error for a video containing the actual technique error. In other words, the system detects a technique error on a video containing the technique error.

A false positive implies that the system predicted a technique issue in a video, when the video did not actually have this technique issue present. Thus, a correct execution of an exercise is predicted as a technique error.

A true negative would occur if a video without any technique issue present is predicted as having no technique issues present. Meaning that a correct execution of an exercise would be predicted as a correct execution.

A false negative would be if the system predicts a video containing a technique issue to be without the technique issue. In other words, a technique error video would be predicted as a correct execution of the exercise.

For this feedback system, the true positive and false positive are the most critical instances. This is because the systems concern themselves with predicting technique aspects present in a video and are not actually predicting which technique aspects that are absent. Thus, making the two predictive terms more relevant.

6.1.2 MODEL TRAINING AND TESTING

The training data are divided into 10 different folds of same size so as the model learns effective mapping of inputs and outputs. The fine tuning and hyper-parameter tuning of features are carried out on these folds. The efficiency of this deep learning is tested using various performance metrics. Table 6.1 and Table 6.2 elaborates the accuracy, specificity, sensitivity, and precision scores across the 10-folds for MobileNet architecture and Inception V3 architecture. The class overlap represents data samples that appear to be valid instances of multiple classes, which could be causing noise in data sets.

The training stops with 10 alternative learning rates, starting with 0.01 for the first hundred, 0.001 for the following hundreds, 0.0001 for the next hundreds, and so on. We repeat this method until we have completed 100 epochs. We take a 0.00001 weight loss into account. Furthermore, in this study we have also compared SGD performance with other training algorithms namely Adagrad, Adadelta, AdamW, and Adamax. Our training and validation of the model consists of two parts: 90% is used for training, 10% is used for validation, and the rest is used for testing.

Folds	Performance Metrics (MobileNet)			
	Specificity	Sensitivity		Precision
Fold-I	98.12	98.17	98.17	98.45
Fold-II	97.24	98.36	98.21	97.41
Fold-III	98.35	97.54	97.27	97.52
Fold-IV	97.46	97.72	97.35	97.36
Fold-V	98.75	97.93	98.74	98.47
Fold-VI	97.52	98.11	98.45	97.69
Fold-VII	98.63	97.13	97.19	96.14
Fold-VIII	97.87	97.74	97.73	97.25
Fold-IX	98.20	97.25	98.46	96.36
Fold-X	97.07	98.36	98.18	96.42
Overlapped Data	NULL	NULL	NULL	NULL
Heat Map Features	98.09	97.14	98.19	98.26
Average	98.11	97.42	98.37	97.75

Table 6.1: Performance Metrics for MobileNet Model

The dataset consists of data from multiple subjects. We split the data into train and test sets based on subjects. Subject-wise split ensures that the specific characteristics of a test subject do not leak into the training set and the performance on the test set can be generalized to any new subject. The suggested architecture's efficiency is estimated using 10-fold cross validation. Figure 6.4 demonstrates the mean accuracy across 10 cross fold validations. As the system accuracy stabilizes after just 80 to 100 epochs, 100 epochs are considered for training in each fold.

Folds	Performance Metrics (InceptionV3)			
	Specificity	Sensitivity	Accuracy	Precision
Fold-I	97.22	97.19	96.19	96.28
Fold-II	96.17	96.30	96.25	96.46
Fold-III	96.48	96.52	96.24	96.66
Fold-IV	96.54	96.72	96.35	96.48
Fold-V	96.81	96.99	96.79	98.15
Fold-VI	96.89	96.19	96.46	96.19
Fold-VII	96.19	96.17	96.18	96.49
Fold-VIII	96.13	96.70	96.71	96.65
Fold-IX	96.16	96.27	96.41	96.81
Fold-X	97.74	96.36	96.11	96.26
Overlapped Data	NULL	NULL	NULL	NULL
Heat Map Features	96.37	96.25	96.20	96.22
Average	96.17	96.35	96.37	96.24

Table 6.2: Performance Metrics for InceptionV3 Model

We execute 69 training iterations before ending validation and store the model weights that resulted in the smallest validation set loss. Note that we split our data into multiple smaller batches since it was too large to transmit to the network all at once. The data is completed in batches of 50, requiring 6 iterations. Early stopping is a form of regularization used to avoid overfitting on the training dataset. Early stopping keeps track of the validation loss, if the loss stops decreasing for several epochs in a row the training stops.

The evaluation dataset consisted of key point data generated from all three pose estimation systems using all 82 videos. For each view and each exercise there is one corresponding video of correct execution of the videos for each user. However, as mentioned, not all the users were able to deliberately perform a squat with a knee extension, leading to only 5 videos created in this category. The total number of files being used in this evaluation is 252, for each pose estimation system this is 82 files.

The goal of the Action Recognition System was to accurately predict the filming angle and perform exercise. This consisted of the two sub-tasks, angle detection and exercise detection. The results of each one is presented independently in Table I and Table II. After determining the viewing angle, the exercise detection algorithm was used to determine what vector calculations to use on the video. The exercise detection was able to detect all true deadlifts, but also predicted 5 false positives, where videos of a squat were wrongfully predicted to be deadlifts. These were squats filmed from the side view, which inherently consisted of key points with fairly low confidence scores. The rest of the 247 files were predicted correctly, resulting in a fairly high accuracy. OpenPose was the only candidate with correct predictions for all of the 84 videos.

The observed average specificity value is 98.11%, average sensitivity is 97.42%, average accuracy is 98.37% and average precision is recorded as 97.75% for the MobileNet architecture. No overlapped data are used to test the model. Figure 6.1 and Figure 6.2 demonstrates the accuracy and loss curves for the MobileNet architectural model. The train and test losses stabilize at 81 epochs where the difference between the two final loss values is negligible, resulting in a well-fit learning curve. Whereas, the observed average specificity value is 96.17%, average sensitivity is 96.35%, average accuracy is 96.37% and average precision is recorded as 96.24% for the InceptionV3 architecture. Figure 6.3 demonstrates the accuracy and loss curves for the InceptionV3 architectural model.

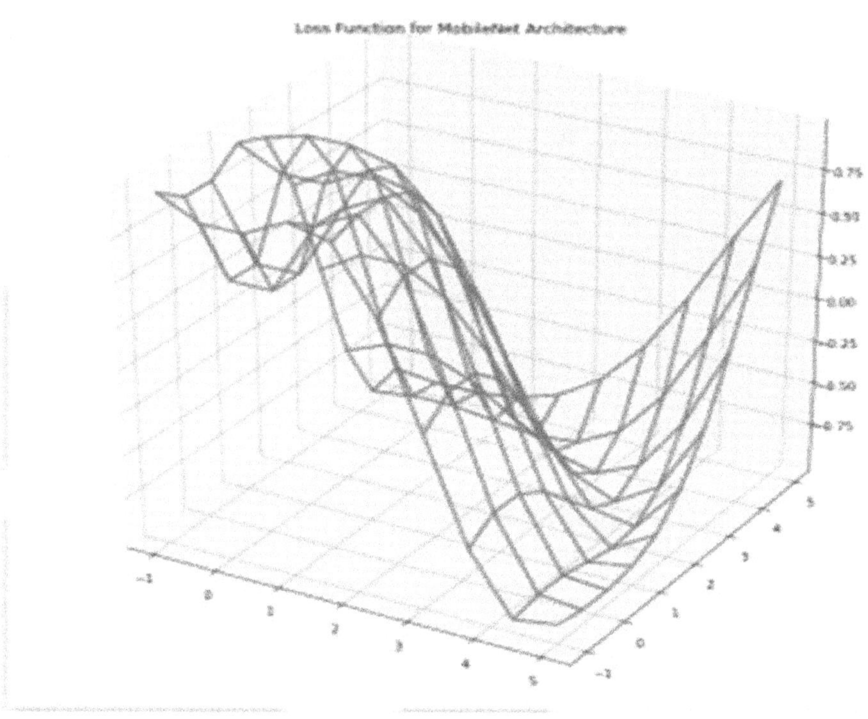

Fig 6.1 Loss Function for MobileNet Architecture on Training and Testing

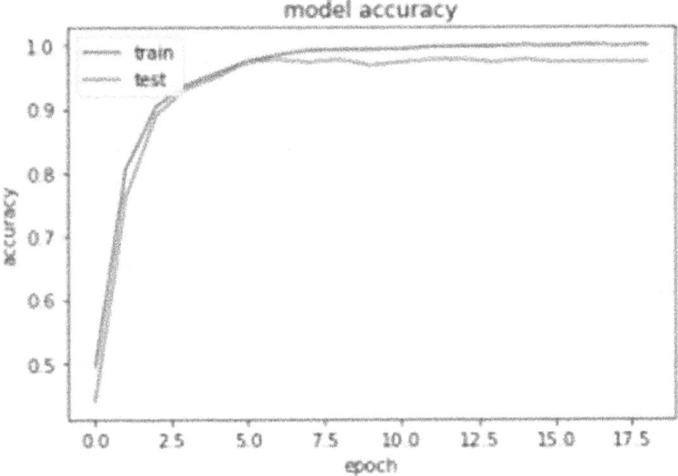

Fig 6.2 Accuracy Curves for MobileNet Architecture on Training and Testing Data

There are a few things that could have been done differently to better evaluate the system. Considering that there are a lot of methods being tested, the dataset would benefit from being considerably larger, by adding more users and even more videos, to better answer the research question of this thesis. Fortunately, the results still seem to point towards a satisfactory conclusion. MobileNet architectural model performs much better as compared with the InceptionV3 in the aspects of Accuracy, Training time, Prediction Time and Model size.

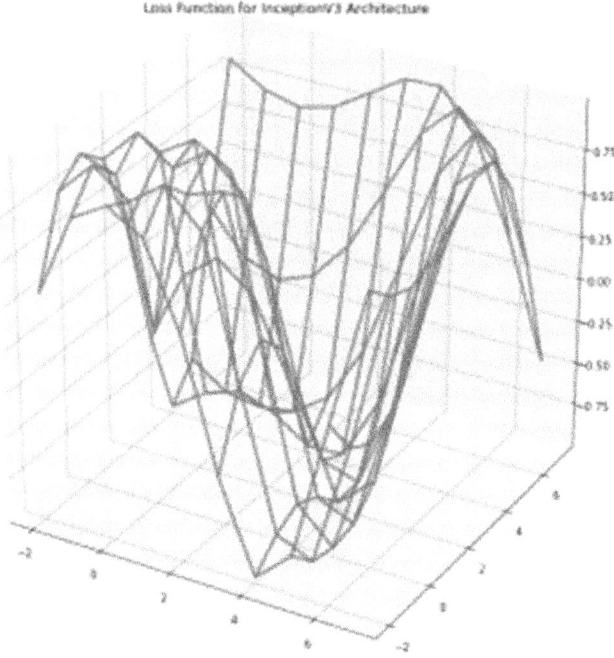

Fig 6.3 Loss Function for InceptionV3 Architecture on Training and Testing

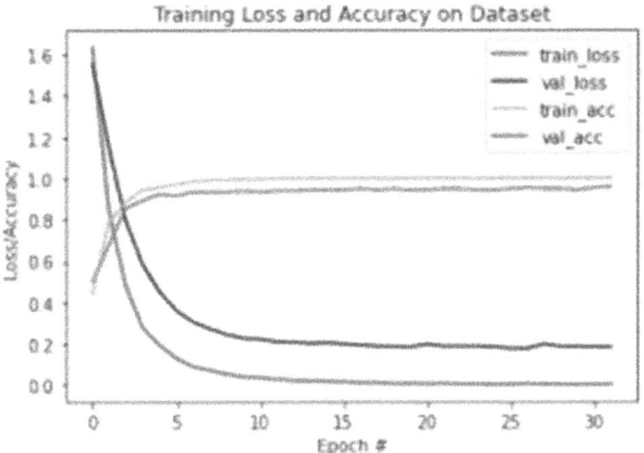

Fig 6.4 Accuracy and Loss Curves for InceptionV3 Architecture on Training and Testing Data

The results shown in Table 6.3 indicate the best fitting effect with the most stable fluctuation in the gradient descent curve is observed for Adamax while training the model. When training the MobileNet model, Adamax is deployed as the optimizer. The results show that Adamax constantly outperforms all other optimizers for the task we selected. On testing accuracies, SGD, Adam, and AdamW come in second, third, and fourth, respectively. After 100 epochs on the testing dataset, the model performance for Adamax, SGD, Adam, and AdamW is equivalent. Adamax and SGD exhibit the most improvement in the first few epochs.

Optimizer	30 Epochs	75 Epochs	150 Epochs	300 Epochs
SGD	17.68 ± 0.19	14.63 ± 0.12	11.04 ± 0.21	14.63 ± 0.12
Adam	17.88 ± 0.17	14.45 ± 0.06	11.07 ± 0.14	14.45 ± 0.06
Adadelta	16.49 ± 0.16	12.37 ± 0.15	11.14 ± 0.16	12.37 ± 0.15
Adagrad	16.51 ± 0.4	15.41 ± 0.20	11.06 ± 0.18	15.41 ± 0.20
Adamw	18.35 ± 0.12	13.67 ± 0.17	11.12 ± 0.10	13.67 ± 0.17
Adamax	10.65 ± 0.05	8.86 ± 0.19	8.02 ± 0.21	8.86 ± 0.19

Table 6.3: Performance of Different Optimizers on Test Data

Also, regarding the goal of the thesis, if users are to use this software, there needs to be an acceptance in the market. Lastly, key points on a 2-D video seem to give valuable information on whether or not the user is performing their exercises with correct form. Though an important aspect of workout is also knowing which muscles to engage, not only if the person is using the correct form. A correct form may increase the likelihood that the correct muscles are being used, but this can only be tracked by other more sophisticated hardware or through user feedback.

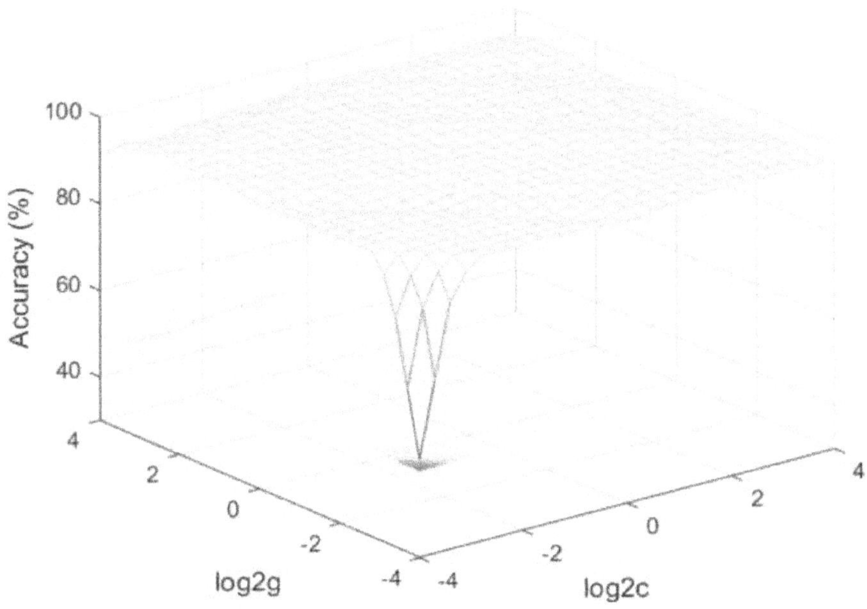

Fig 6.5 Mean Accuracy Plot across 10-Fold Cross Validation

The findings indicate that 2D Human Pose Estimation may be successful in giving feedback on weight training techniques to minimize risk of injuries from a front viewing angle on healthy individuals. Further research and improvement to the technique detection is needed to better answer if the success of front view is transferable to side viewing angles. The favorable results from the Pose Trainer on side viewing angles might also suggest that dynamic time warping is a better choice for these types of technique aspects. Exercises that require rotation seem to be harder to detect, but the system is able to generate partially successful results here.

Activity	True Positives	False Positives
Triceps Pushdown	0.98	0.02
Push Up	0.99	0.01
Lat Pulldown	1.00	0.00
Incline Bench Press	0.98	0.02
Deadlift	1.00	0.00
Chest Fly Machine	0.97	0.03
Biceps Curl	0.97	0.03
Bench Press	0.99	0.01

Table 6.4: True Positive and False Positive Classification for Test Dataset using MobileNet Architecture

Table 6.4 shows the classification rate of each activity performed by an individual with true positives and false positives. These outcomes show the rate of correct and incorrect classification of data sample indicating the performance of model. Pose Trainer achieved good results using their machine learning approach, with front raise being correctly detected as either correct or incorrect for all exercises. The other exercises also showed good results with a F1 score around the 0.8 mark. This data however, is only the result of the machine learning approach. As for the geometric algorithm used, none of the results were mentioned except for the bicep curl detector which was able to detect 80% of the bad executions. The bicep curl, front rise and shoulder press were all detected from a side view perspective, and gave considerable higher scores than the side view evaluation in this thesis. This reveals that dynamic time warping may be a better choice for this scenario.

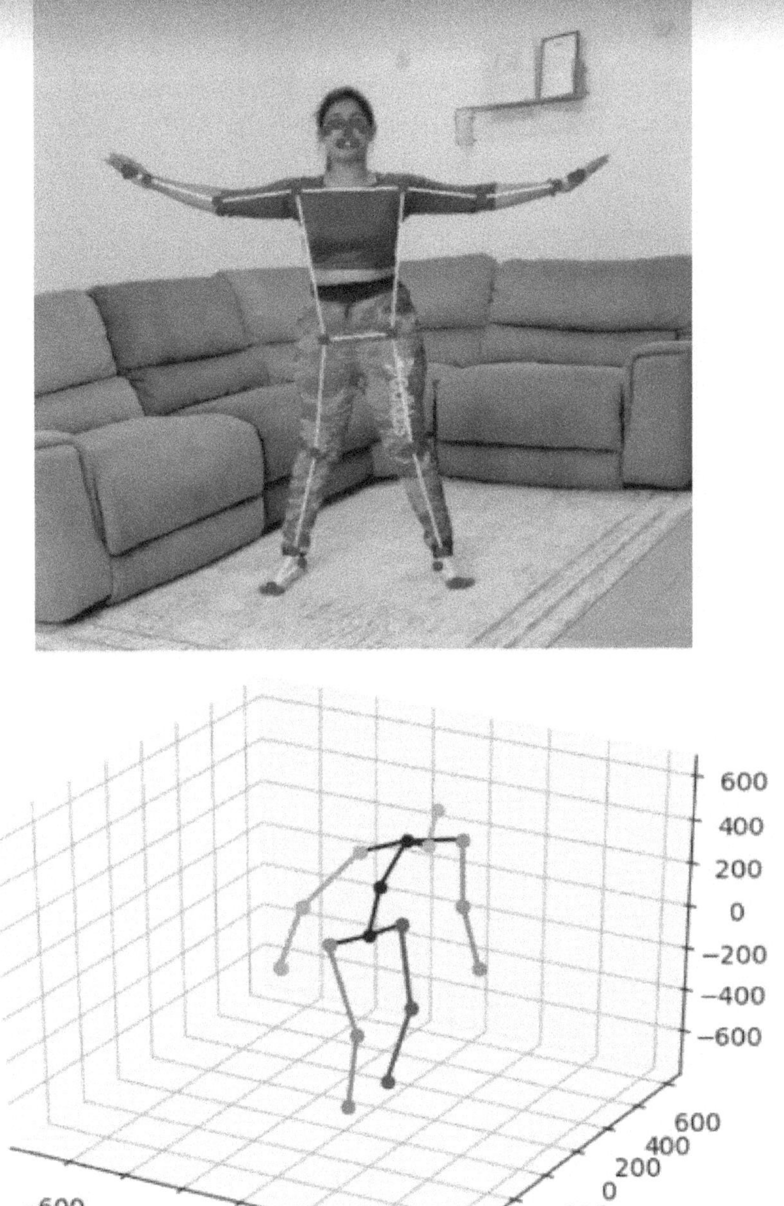

Fig 6.6 3D Plot for Pose Estimation across a Workout Activity

6.2 DISCUSSION

Comparing these findings to the Pose Trainer, the system at hand seems to generate similar results, yet with a larger dataset and more precise feedback on more complex exercises. This research extends what has been done in Pose Trainer and confidently shows how well simple techniques used with 2D Human Pose Estimation key points can give feedback on weight lifting form. While using the same metrics to evaluate the results, Pose Trainer presented the data with regards to correct or incorrect execution of the movements. While this thesis presents the result for each given technique aspect separately, which in turn makes the results challenging to compare to one another.

To be able to give feedback on weight training technique, it is crucial to know which angle the exercise is being filmed from. This is the first decisive step in analyzing the exercise videos, a wrong angle prediction would lead to wrong results throughout the rest of the system. By using a distance vector between both shoulders the system was able to accurately predict all viewing angles without any error. The distance between the shoulders of a person is very consistent, independent of what movement the user is doing. This suggests that larger datasets of the same composition of front and side viewing angles will achieve similar results.

The loss, as mentioned in the methodology section, were a result of too low confidence score leading to inaccurate calculations. Even though the confidence thresholds were the same for every pose estimation system, some lead to more errors than others. The confidence output of every system might be using a different scale, meaning that a confidence score of 0.9 on AlphaPose might not be the same as a 0.9 score on OpenPose. This might also explain the higher scores on OpenPose, as they may be stricter on what a confidence score of 0.9 is, leading to more errors under calculation. It would be interesting to see if AlphaPose and OpenPose had similar results if the confidence threshold was lowered for OpenPose, thereby removing the errors. The dataset consisted of a very narrow user base, consisting only of healthy young individuals with some amateur lifting experience. This might discriminate towards users with physical disabilities or body types that largely diverge from the dataset generated in this thesis.

In addition to gaining insight into different Human Pose Estimation Systems and researching risk related to weight training, two physical systems were decided on to try answering the research question. A Action Recognition System with the goal of automatically detecting the exercise and filming angle of a video, such that the technique aspects related to the given exercise and filming angle can be automatically tested for. And a Technique Evaluation System with the goal of detecting technique aspects with a high association to risk of injury. Thereby informing the users when they are performing an exercise in such a manner that they risk injuring themselves.

The angle detector has not been tested for angles that are not necessarily categorized as being strictly front or side. The system cannot rule out angles that are not supported by the vector calculations. Since the system is using the average non-normalized distance between the shoulders, any movement that involves excessive rotations of the user will increase the likelihood of false predictions. The squat and the deadlift restrict the user from rotating excessively, but other complex exercises might prove to be challenging. Since the shoulders are not normalized for this detection method, a person very far away from the camera doing a front viewing exercise, will possibly have a perceived shoulder distance small enough to be predicted by the system as being filmed from the side. The average shoulder distance was compared against a constant threshold value, which is independent of how much space the user is taking up from the image.

CHAPTER SEVEN

CONCLUSION

7.1 CONCLUSION

This research aimed at using Human Pose Estimation to capture and detect specific technique related issues in daily workouts. By testing multiple Human Pose Estimation systems on a small set of users, the thesis has shown that the technology can be applied to create a working fitness technique evaluation system for multiple users, exercises and technique issues.

The research clearly illustrates that Pose Estimation technology can be accurate enough to detect technique issues in weight lifting, but it also raises the question about its possibility to detect issues only visible from the side. The inaccuracy of the Pose Estimation tools on side view videos impacts the rest of the solution to perform significantly better on videos seen from the front than the side.

While the small user set limits the generalizability of the results, this approach provides new insight by testing the same solution for different body compositions and multiple pose extraction systems. Proving that variations can be accounted for and generalized such that inferences about weight lifting technique can be performed correctly. Earlier work in the area has mainly focused on depth cameras or multiple sensors to gain information in the three-dimensional space.

This thesis explored the two-dimensional space by only using a single RGB camera to capture the pose of the subject. This resulted in a more accessibility service, that theoretically requires no more than a mobile camera of the users themselves. This thesis also separates from earlier work by detecting specific technique issues instead of exclusively distinguishing between correct and incorrect execution of an exercise.

60

This thesis also separates from earlier work by detecting specific technique issues instead of exclusively distinguishing between correct and incorrect execution of an exercise. By attacking the problem in this manner, we have more information on precisely what the users are doing wrong during an exercise.

Thus, giving ourselves the opportunity to provide the user with feedback on what they have to change in order to fix their form for that exercise. This is an important aspect to minimize the risk of injury, which this system is all about.

CHAPTER EIGHT

FUTURE SCOPE

8.1 FUTURE SCOPE

Based on these conclusions, practitioners should consider testing the same approach on a bigger user set, with higher variability between experience and body composition to confirm the findings of this thesis. An approach where the users themselves film and provide footage for testing could reveal issues not observed in a controlled environment, as well as help maximize the diversity in the dataset. Further work should also include adding to the exercise and technique pool to explore the transferability of the solution to other exercises.

Since the specific technique issues are known, it is possible to build on the solution to provide specific feedback for improvement to the user. This could simply be the detected aspect or more detailed information as which knee moves inward or which way the hips rotate. A description on how to improve the technique issue could also be presented as feedback, provided the domain knowledge is present.

Another improvement is to use the relative height of the person in the time series to track the subject's movements during an exercise. By doing so, the start and stop position of a repetition can be automatically defined and repetitions counted. This dismisses the need to manually define the start and end position of a movement.

The improvements mentioned above are not only interesting topics for further research, but added all together, they have the opportunity to form a complete application with interface, technique evaluation and feedback to the user. An application to guide the users towards an injury free lifting experience, all with the Human Pose Estimation Assisted Fitness Technique Evaluation System at the core of the application.

CHAPTER NINE

REFERENCES

[1] H. Xiong, S. Berkovsky, R. V. Sharan, S. Liu, and E. Coiera, "Robust vision based workout analysis using diversified deep latent variable model," in 2020 42nd Annual International Conference of the IEEE Engineering in Medicine Biology Society (EMBC), pp. 2155–2158, 2020.

[2] S. Yadav, A. Singh, A. Gupta, and J. Raheja, "Real-time yoga recognition using deep learning," Neural Computing and Applications, vol. 31, pp. https://link.springer.com/article/10.1007/s00521–019, 12 2019.

[3] Y. Gu, S. Pandit, E. Saraee, T. Nordahl, T. Ellis, and M. Betke, "Home-based physical therapy with an interactive computer vision system," in 2019 IEEE/CVF International Conference on Computer Vision Workshop (ICCVW), pp. 2619–2628, 2019.

[4] C. Huang, Y.-Z. He, and C.-C. Hsu, "Computer-assisted yoga training system," Multimedia Tools and Applications, vol. 77, 09 2018.

[5] S. Chen and R. Yang, "Pose trainer: Correcting exercise posture using pose estimation," 03 2018.

[6] P. Keshari, "Wrong posture detection using opencv and support vector machine," 01 2020.

[7] A. Nagarkoti, R. Teotia, A. K. Mahale, and P. K. Das, "Realtime indoor workout analysis using machine learning amp; computer vision," in 2019 41st Annual International Conference of the IEEE Engineering in Medicine and Biology Society (EMBC), pp. 1440– 1443, 2019.

[8] Y. Agrawal, Y. Shah, and A. Sharma, "Implementation of machine learning technique for identification of yoga poses," in 2020 IEEE 9th International Conference on Communication Systems and Network Technologies (CSNT), pp. 40–43, 2020.

[9] Z. Cao, G. Hidalgo, T. Simon, S. Wei, and Y. Sheikh, "Openpose: Realtime multi person 2d pose estimation using part affinity fields," IEEE

Transactions on Pattern Analysis & Machine Intelligence, vol. 43, pp. 172–186, jan 2021.

[10] D. Kumar and A. Sinha, "Yoga pose detection and classification using deep learning," International Journal of Scientific Research in Computer Science Engineering and Information Technology, 11 2020.

[11] G. Chiddarwar, A. Ranjane, M. Chindhe, R. Deodhar, and P. Gangamwar, "Aibased yoga pose estimation for android application," International Journal of Innovative Science and Research Technology, vol. 5, pp. 1070–1073, 10 2020.

[12] Q. Dang, J. Yin, B. Wang, and W. Zheng, "Deep learning based 2d human pose estimation: A survey," Tsinghua Science and Technology, vol. 24, no. 6, pp. 663– 676, 2019.

[13] F. Sajjad, A. F. Ahmed, and M. A. Ahmed, "A study on the learning based human pose recognition," in 2017 9th IEEE-GCC Conference and Exhibition (GCCCE), pp. 1–8, 2017.

[14] H.-T. Chen, Y.-Z. He, and C.-C. Hsu, "Computer-assisted yoga training system," Multimedia Tools and Applications, vol. 77, no. 18, pp. 23969–23991, 2018.

[15] S. Jain, A. Rustagi, S. Saurav, R. Saini, and S. Singh, "Three dimensional CNN inspired deep learning architecture for Yoga pose recognition in the real-world environment," Neural Computational Intelligence and Neuroscience, Computing & Applications, vol. 33, no. 12, pp. 6427–6441, 2021.

[16] Mais Yasen and Shaidah Jusoh. "A systematic review on hand gesture recognition techniques, challenges and applications". In: PeerJ Computer Science 5 (2019), e218

[17] H. Tang, Q. Wang and H. Chen, "Research on 3D Human Pose Estimation Using RGBD Camera," 2019 IEEE 9th International Conference on Electronics Information and Emergency Communication (ICEIEC), 2019, pp. 538-541, doi: 10.1109/ICEIEC.2019.8784591.

[18] G.R.S. Murthy and R.s Jadon. "A review of vision based hand gesture recognition". In: International Journal of Information Technology and Knowledge Management 2 (Aug. 2), pp. 405–410

[19] Santiago Riofrio et al. "Gesture Recognition Using Dynamic Time Warping and Kinect: A Practical Approach". In: Nov. 2017, pp. 302–308. doi: 10 . 1109/INCISCOS.2017.36. .

[20] Zhe Cao et al. "OpenPose: Realtime Multi-Person 2D Pose Estimation Using Part Affinity Fields". In: IEEE Transactions on Pattern

Analysis and Machine Intelligence 43.1 (2021), pp. 172–186. doi: 10.1109/ TPAMI.2019.2929257.

[21] T. L. Munea, Y. Z. Jembre, H. T. Weldegebriel, L. Chen, C. Huang and C. Yang, "The Progress of Human Pose Estimation: A Survey and Taxonomy of Models Applied in 2D Human Pose Estimation," in IEEE Access, vol. 8, pp. 133330-133348, 2020, doi: 10.1109/ ACCESS.2020.3010248.

[22] Y. Cheng, P. Yi, R. Liu, J. Dong, D. Zhou and Q. Zhang, "Human-robot Interaction Method Combining Human Pose Estimation and Motion Intention Recognition," 2021 IEEE 24th International Conference on Computer Supported Cooperative Work in Design (CSCWD), 2021, pp. 958-963, doi: 10.1109/CSCWD49262.2021.9437772.

[23] Imam Riadi, Sunardi Sunardi, and Arizona Firmansyah. "Forensic Investigation Technique on Android's Blackberry Messenger using NIST Framework". In: International Journal of Cyber-Security and Digital Forensics 6 (Oct. 2017), pp. 198–205.

[24] Henrik Sj¨oberg et al. "Content Validity Index and Reliability of a New Protocol for Evaluation of Lifting Technique in the Powerlifting Squat and Deadlift". In: Journal of Strength and Conditioning Research (Sept. 2018). doi: 10.1519/ JSC.0000000000002791.

[25] Zhe Cao et al. "OpenPose: Realtime Multi-Person 2D Pose Estimation using Part Affinity Fields". In: (Dec. 2018).

[26] S. Parajuli and M. K. Guragai, "Human Pose Estimation in 3D using heatmaps," 2022 2nd International Conference on Artificial Intelligence and Signal Processing (AISP), 2022, pp. 1-4, doi: 10.1109/ AISP53593.2022.9760634.

[27] Pose Detection comparison : wrnchAI vs OpenPose. https://www.learnopencv. com/pose-detection-comparison-wrnchai-vs-openpose/. Accessed: 2020- 01-29.

[28] Dushyant Mehta et al. XNect: Real-time Multi-person 3D Human Pose Estimation with a Single RGB Camera. July 2019.

[29] D. -h. Kong and S. -j. Kang, "Downsizing Heatmap Resolution for real-time 3D Human Pose Estimation," 2021 36th International Technical Conference on Circuits/Systems, Computers and Communications (ITC-CSCC), 2021, pp. 1-4, doi: 10.1109/ITC-CSCC52171.2021.9501409.

[30] G. Dsouza, D. Maurya and A. Patel, "Smart gym trainer using Human pose estimation," 2020 IEEE International Conference for Innovation in Technology (INOCON), 2020, pp. 1-4, doi: 10.1109/

INOCON50539.2020.9298212.

[31] Dushyant Mehta et al. "VNect". In: ACM Transactions on Graphics 36.4 (July 2017), pp. 1–14. issn: 0730-0301. doi: 10 . 1145 / 3072959 . 3073596. url: http://dx.doi.org/10.1145/3072959.3073596.

[32] Laxman Kumarapu and Prerana Mukherjee. AnimePose: Multi-person 3D pose estimation and animation. 2020. arXiv: 2002.02792 [cs.GR].

[33] Christian Zimmermann et al. 3D Human Pose Estimation in RGBD Images for Robotic Task Learning. 2018. arXiv: 1803.02622 [cs.CV].

[34] S. Wang, H. Ai, T. Yamashita and S. Lao, "Combined Top-Down/ Bottom-Up Human Articulated Pose Estimation Using AdaBoost Learning," 2010 20th International Conference on Pattern Recognition, 2010, pp. 3670-3673, doi: 10.1109/ICPR.2010.895.

[35] Adri`a Arbu´es-Sang¨uesa, Coloma Ballester, and Gloria Haro. Single-Camera Basketball Tracker through Pose and Semantic Feature Fusion. 2019. arXiv: 1906.02042 [cs.CV].

[36] D. Singh, S. Panthri and P. Venkateshwari, "Human Body Parts Measurement using Human Pose Estimation," 2022 9th International Conference on Computing for Sustainable Global Development (INDIACom), 2022, pp. 288-292, doi: 10.23919/ INDIACom54597.2022.9763292.

[37] Lewis Bridgeman et al. "Multi-Person 3D Pose Estimation and Tracking in Sports". In: CVPR Workshops. 2019.

[38] E. Nishani and B. Çiço, "Computer vision approaches based on deep learning and neural networks: Deep neural networks for video analysis of human pose estimation," 2017 6th Mediterranean Conference on Embedded Computing (MECO), 2017, pp. 1-4, doi: 10.1109/MECO.2017.7977207.

[39] Kaiming He et al. "Mask R-CNN". In: 2017 IEEE International Conference on Computer Vision (ICCV) (2017), pp. 2980–2988.

[40] George Papandreou et al. Towards Accurate Multi-person Pose Estimation in the Wild. 2017. arXiv: 1701.01779 [cs.CV].

[41] Sun Ke et al. "Deep High-Resolution Representation Learning for Human Pose Estimation". In: (Feb. 2019).

[42] Yilun Chen et al. "Cascaded Pyramid Network for Multi-person Pose Estimation". In: June 2018, pp. 7103–7112. doi: 10.1109/ CVPR.2018.00742.

[43] M. Patel and N. Kalani, "A Comparative Analysis for Single Person and Multi Person Pose Estimation Using Deep Learning Algorithms," 2021 International Conference on Circuits, Controls and Communications

(CCUBE), 2021, pp. 1-5, doi: 10.1109/CCUBE53681.2021.9702744.

[44] K. Toyoda, M. Kono and J. Rekimoto, "Post-Data Augmentation to Improve Deep Pose Estimation of Extreme and Wild Motions," 2019 IEEE Conference on Virtual Reality and 3D User Interfaces (VR), 2019, pp. 1570-1574, doi: 10.1109/VR.2019.8798221.

[45] George Papandreou et al. "PersonLab: Person Pose Estimation and Instance Segmentation with a Bottom-Up, Part-Based, Geometric Embedding Model". In: ECCV. 2018.

[46] Muhammed Kocabas, Salih Karagoz, and Emre Akbas. "MultiPoseNet: Fast Multi Person Pose Estimation Using Pose Residual Network: 15th European Conference, Munich, Germany, September 8-14, 2018, Proceedings, Part XI". In: Sept. 2018, pp. 437– 453. isbn: 978-3-030-01251-9. doi: 10.1007/978-3- 030-01252-6_26.

[47] L. Cai and W. Liu, "Multi-stage network based on connected simple backbone interaction for human pose estimation," 2021 IEEE International Conference on Artificial Intelligence and Computer Applications (ICAICA), 2021, pp. 863-866, doi: 10.1109/ICAICA52286.2021.9498117.

[48] H. -Y. Lin, T. -W. Chen, C. -C. Chen, C. -H. Hsieh and W. -N. Lie, "Human pose estimation from monocular image captures," 2009 IEEE International Conference on Multimedia and Expo, 2009, pp. 994-997, doi: 10.1109/ICME.2009.5202664.

[49] Carlos Caetano et al. "Magnitude-Orientation Stream network and depth information applied to activity recognition". In: Journal of Visual Communication and Image Representation 63 (Aug. 2019), p. 102596. issn: 10473203. doi: 10.1016/ j.jvcir.2019.102596

[50] Dhawas, P., Ramteke, M. A., Thakur, A., Polshetwar, P. V., Salunkhe, R. V., & Bhagat, D. (2024). Big Data Analysis Techniques: Data Preprocessing Techniques, Data Mining Techniques, Machine Learning Algorithm, Visualization. In Big Data Analytics Techniques for Market Intelligence (pp. 183-208). IGI Global.

[51] Dhawas, P., Dhore, A., Bhagat, D., Pawar, R. D., Kukade, A., & Kalbande, K. (2024). Big Data Preprocessing, Techniques, Integration, Transformation, Normalisation, Cleaning, Discretization, and Binning. In Big Data Analytics Techniques for Market Intelligence (pp. 159-182). IGI Global.

[52] Dhawas, P., Kolhe, P., Khan, F., Chauragade, L., & Dhimole, A. (2022). Document Analyser Using Deep Learning.

About Authors

PROF. PRANALI DHAWAS

DEPARTMENT OF ARTIFICIAL INTELLIGENCEG H RAISONI COLLEGE
OF ENGINEERING, NAGPUR

Pranali Dhawas, an accomplished educator and technologist, is dedicated to teaching and staying updated on emerging technologies. With a wealth of experience, she has made substantial contributions to education, spanning teaching, research, and innovative projects. She has a 3-year professional background, previously affiliated with RTMNU Nagpur University and currently working at G H Raisoni College of Engineering, Nagpur since 2022. Driven by a commitment to knowledge sharing, Prof. Pranali Dhawas has authored and significantly contributed to diverse books and research papers, including topics like Machine Learning, Data Analytics, Big data, Data Pre-processing and Natural Language Processing. Her papers are published in reputable journals like Scopus, reflecting her dedication to expanding knowledge boundaries. Prof. Pranali's skills extend beyond teaching to encompass technical proficiency.

MS. BHARGAVI KAKIRWAR Artificial Intelligence Engineer |
MBA(Business Analytics & Marketing) MIT-WPU'RSoL

Bhargavi Kakirwar is an accomplished author and professional with a strong background in both technology and business. She holds a Bachelor of Technology in Artificial Intelligence and a Master of Business Administration in Business Analytics and Marketing. Additionally, she has certifications in leadership, strategy, and business English. Bhargavi's expertise extends beyond academia into the realms of startups and non-profit organizations, where she has gained valuable experience. She has been recognized for her contributions to women entrepreneurship and empowerment, receiving the Lilawati Award. Bhargavi's research has been published in prestigious international journals and conferences, highlighting her commitment to advancing knowledge in the fields of technology and business synergy.

MR. TANMAY HANDE Artificial Intelligence Engineer |
MBA(Business Analytics & Marketing) MIT-WPU'RSoL

Tanmay Hande is a skilled author specializing in Artificial Intelligence, blending technical expertise with business insight. He holds a background as an Artificial Intelligence Engineer and is currently pursuing an MBA in Business Analytics and Marketing. With a Certification of Leadership and Strategy from INSEAD, Tanmay approaches problem-solving and innovation comprehensively. His expertise covers various AI domains such as Natural Language Processing, Deep Learning, Machine Learning, and Image Recognition. Beyond academia, Tanmay has published in prestigious journals and presented at conferences, aiming to simplify AI concepts for broader understanding. He is now exploring the AI landscape, merging technical prowess with strategic insight to drive innovation and progress.

MR. AADITYA GUPTA Artificial Intelligence Engineer | Masters in
Management at Dublin, Ireland

Aaditya Abhijeet Gupta is a versatile postgraduate student pursuing
a Masters in Management at the esteemed University College Dublin,
leveraging a background in engineering and artificial intelligence. With
a commitment to social work, he actively engaged with NGOs and
collaborated with the local government during the COVID-19 lockdown
in India. Aaditya brings a wealth of professional experience, including
internships in digital marketing and cooperative banking, showcasing
adaptability and resilience. Aaditya's achievements extend to martial arts,
with gold medals in SQAY and kickboxing at state and national levels.
His vision includes to create employment opportunities and foster local
development across his hometown.